Do Not Disturb

A Comedy

Michael Pertwee

Samuel French – London
New York – Sydney – Toronto – Hollywood

CHARACTERS

Jay
Darlene
Sonia
Rose
Mary

The action of the play takes place in a studio flat in North-West London

Time — the present

AUTHOR'S NOTE

Jay must be at least forty years of age but he could be fifteen years older. Only a few lines have to be changed to suit any age between forty and fifty-five. The character of Rose must be cast to suit the age of the actor playing Jay.

ACT ONE

A studio flat in North-West London. Late afternoon

It is a one-room apartment, which includes a bedroom alcove. There are three doors—a front door, a door to the bathroom and a door to the kitchen. It is expensively and tastefully decorated, but the decorations are not entirely complete. One section of wall has not been papered, and rolls of paper, pots of paint and a step ladder are evidence of incompleted work. The furniture is expensive, comfortable and in good taste. There is ample evidence that the occupier has only just moved in, including an open and unpacked suitcase, and a tea chest, filled with objects wrapped in newspaper. UR is a square alcove, which houses a round bed, with pillows, a sheet and a duvet on it. The rear wall is taken up with a range of fitted cupboards. On the R wall is a single, sash window. The alcove can be concealed from view by curtains which are opened and closed by a remote control instrument, similar to that which operates TV sets. In the UR corner is a small round table, with a lamp on it. The alcove, and an area below the curtains, are on a rostrum. This rostrum is carpeted. Further down, in the centre of the R wall, is a double-sashed window, set in a small alcove. Through all the windows, houses on the opposite side of the street can be seen. Opposite the double window, and still on the rostrum, is a round dining-table and four chairs. DR is the door to the bathroom, which opens inwards. To the L of the alcove in the rear wall, and set some feet further downstage than the rear wall of the alcove, is the front door, which opens into the room. It has a letter-box in it. When the door is open, it is possible for the audience to see a landing. To the L of this landing is a bannister belonging to the staircase. Across the landing is the front door to another flat. To the L of the front door is a fitment of shelves, which houses hi-fi equipment, a clock, books, various ornaments and other objects, carelessly arranged. On the L wall is a door to the kitchen. When open, a section of the kitchen may be seen. DS of the kitchen door, against the wall, is a desk on which is a push-button phone, some telephone directories, tumblers, a bottle of gin, a bottle of whisky, a pencil and paper, a pocket tape-recorder. DSR is a pouffe. Centre stage, facing the audience is a comfortable, low-backed sofa. To the L of the sofa is a large, square coffee table. DSL is an armchair

When the Curtain *rises Jay Spencer is discovered on the phone, half sitting on the desk, facing* R. *Jay is somewhere into middle-age, and would readily agree he does not look it. He is casually dressed*

Jay (*on the phone*) We'll go with a nice plant, I think. An azalea would be fine. ... A card? Yes. ... "Thanks. You were gr——" No, scrub that. Sorry. Just put: "Well! Well! Well! Who'd have thought it?" That's all. ... No. No signature. (*Opening a wallet and searching for a credit card*) J for

Jason Spencer, with a C. I'll pay by American Express. (*Searching among several cards*) I won't pay by American Express. I seem to have lost it. You take Barclaycard? (*Picking up a Barclaycard, and squinting at it a bit myopically*) F, four-eight-three-seven-eight-one-o-two-one. . . . Yes, delivery tomorrow morning will be fine. Bye. (*He hangs up, replaces the cards and frowns. He picks up the pocket tape-recorder from the desk, switches it on and talks into it*) Miss Parfitt. I seem to have mislaid my American Express card. Is it anywhere in the office?

He wanders R, *looking around, perhaps slightly shifting the position of the armchair on the way. He mounts the rostrum and approaches the dining-table. He leaves the recorder on the table, and picks up the control instrument which operates the curtains at the alcove. He presses a button. The curtains start to close with a pleasant hum. He presses another button and they open again. He enjoys this. He lies down on the bed and starts to close the curtains. We hear the sound of a loud female sneeze from the direction of the front door. Jay stops the curtains*

The front door opens very slowly and Darlene puts her head in. She cannot see Jay

Darlene is pretty, waifish, downbeat and probably still in her teens. She is barefoot, and wears nothing but a large, man's shirt, disturbingly unbuttoned. She clutches a paper tissue to her nose. She glances round the room then, watched in silent fascination by Jay, she moves L *towards the kitchen door. What ensues will instantly convey to the audience that this is a girl who is accident prone. She pauses by the fitment, and seems to be searching for something on the shelves. She upsets an ornament, just rescues it from falling to the ground but, in so doing, knocks an expensive-looking clock to the ground. She picks it up and shakes it, then listens to see if it still ticks. It makes a noise which indicates that its works are now in many pieces. She replaces the clock and steps back. In so doing she evidently treads on a pile of plates, concealed from view by the armchair. She bends down and picks up a plate which is broken in two pieces. She wonders what to do; considers concealing them behind a cushion in the chair, decides against this, and settles on concealing the two pieces under the chair*

Darlene exits into the kitchen, knocking over something on the way

From the kitchen comes the crash of something else breaking. This brings Jay to his feet and out of the alcove

Darlene comes out of the kitchen and heads back towards the front door

How do you do.

Darlene gives a start and sees him. Her mouth opens but she says nothing

(*Approaching her*) We haven't met, have we? (*Taking in her attire*) Chilly weather for . . . (*He leans forward politely to listen*)

Darlene lets out a tremendous sneeze

(*Rocking back on his heels*) Bless you! That's a nasty cold you're offering me.

Darlene (*wiping her nose*) Nrr a crr. Aeriery. Ayus.
Jay I didn't catch that.
Darlene Not a cold. Allergy. Sinus.
Jay That's a relief.

Darlene sneezes

  (*Wincing*) One doesn't catch sinus, does one?

Darlene sneezes again

  I hope.
Darlene How are you off for money?
Jay (*in a slightly Jewish accent*) I'm comfortable.
Darlene Can you let me have some?
Jay Ah. There we have a problem. My accountant gets extremely angry with
  me if I loan ...
Darlene (*producing a pound note from the breast pocket of her shirt, and
  proffering it*) I need some change, some ten p's.
Jay Oh! Ah! (*Patting his pockets*) Afraid I can't help.
Darlene For the gas meter. I want to use the oven.
Jay (*turning out both pockets*) Nothing. See? Terribly sorry.
Darlene You got a razor?
Jay You want to shave? I have, but I'm a little fussy about lending it to
  strangers and, anyway, I don't know if the plug fits here.
Darlene Not electric. (*Making a somewhat lethal gesture*) A razor with
  blades.
Jay No. I gave them up shortly after I first married. Women do strange
  things with razors. They only have to look for them and they go blunt.
Darlene What about a kitchen knife, sharp, with a point?
Jay I honestly wouldn't advise trying to shave with a kitchen knife. (*Looking
  at her closely*) You don't need a shave, anyway.
Darlene (*grimly*) It's not for shaving.
Jay Good, but I'm afraid it's no again. I'm just moving in and only have the
  bare essentials.
Darlene What about a bread knife?
Jay No. Not being very helpful, am I?
Darlene (*turning to leave*) No sweat.
Jay Are you collecting information for some census?
Darlene No. I'm staying across the hall.
Jay With no bread knife.
Darlene I use sliced bread.
Jay A very good reason for not having a bread knife, and you're better off
  than me ... I don't even have any bread.

Darlene moves back towards the front door

Darlene (*turning and looking around*) You've done a lot in here haven't you?
Jay Not as much as I'd planned. (*Indicating the unfinished section of wall*)
  My builder's disappeared on the job.
Darlene When did you get here?

Jay About an hour ago.

Darlene (*nodding*) You dropped something didn't you?

Jay That tea chest—on my foot. I hope my language didn't carry?

Darlene (*nodding again*) Yes. The man who lived here before was a pervert.

Jay Was he?

Darlene He did rude things at the top of the stairs—and once out of that window.

Jay You'll be relieved to hear that isn't one of my failings.

Darlene Are you retired?

Jay From doing rude things out of windows?

Darlene From work.

Jay (*looking hurt*) Do I look that old? Don't answer that. No. I still totter in to my business.

Darlene What do you do, then?

Jay I'm a communications consultant, a hydra-headed beast combining PR—that's Public Relations—with Advertising and Motivation Research.

Darlene You sell something?

Jay No, I force the public to buy what it doesn't want, at a price it can't afford. That's the PR side.

Darlene (*blankly*) Huh?

Jay The Motivation Researcher probes your subconscious mind because, more often than not, you have no idea why you buy a particular brand. If I discover what motivates you then I steer you safely in the wrong direction. A shameful trade which I am shortly abandoning for good.

Darlene I don't know what you're talking about.

Jay Put simply, I might persuade you that Daz is a much squarer deal than Square Deal Surf.

Darlene Oh, you're in washing powders.

Jay Brainwashing.

Darlene My dad was a commercial traveller, too.

Before Jay can correct her on this, Darlene gives a slight wave and exits through the front door, almost shutting it behind her

Jay Too? (*He goes to the front door*)

The door opens and Darlene re-appears

Darlene You wouldn't have an axe, or a gun?

Jay (*after a short pause*) No, I wouldn't. One of my reasons for moving in here was to try and put thoughts of murder permanently behind me.

Darlene gives a little "tck" of irritation and exits

(*Imitating her "tck" and closing the front door*) Axe? Gun?

The doorbell rings

(*Mimicking Darlene*) What about an Exocet missile? (*He throws open the door. He freezes slightly but his face remains expressionless. He stands back*)

Sonia enters. She is in her late twenties, dressed to accentuate a voluptuous figure. She carries a handbag. She has a penchant for large costume jewellery. She looks, and is, a starlet. She has a somewhat schizoid personality, one moment a violent, extremely foul-mouthed child, the next intelligent and reasonably articulate

Sonia And what, precisely, is all this?

Jay Precisely, Flat Four, Twenty-Two, Pottersby Road, NW Three, Seven, AA. Studio apartment of character with exceptional view over Primrose Hill, a distant glimpse of St John's Wood and, with the aid of binoculars, Willesden, or is it Neasden? I hope it's Willesden. I've always loathed the sound of Neasden.

She lights a cigarette. Her movements betray pent-up nerves

Sonia Inane chatter won't put me off, or aren't I entitled to ask why I find you holed up in what I assume is some kind of love nest?

Jay Definitely entitled.

Sonia Thank you. So, about this dump, whose is it?

Jay Until two thousand and one—mine.

Sonia You setting someone up here?

Jay No. Well, yes—me. (*After a short pause*) I've left you, Sonia.

Sonia Just like that? Without a word? Or did I miss a farewell note on the mantelpiece?

Jay (*shaking his head*) It seemed—tidier this way.

Sonia Tidier! That is the most despicable, cowardly thing I ever heard.

Jay (*nodding*) Yes, but I've always been a coward where you're concerned.

Sonia You can't seriously have intended to disappear?

Jay Of course not, but the first step was to summon up the courage to make the break. How did you find me? Is there a mole in my office?

Sonia Betrayed by the perfect Miss Parfitt? No! That cow is well cowed. You've been acting oddly for weeks, so ... (*a trifle nervously*) I hired a private detective.

Jay (*startled*) Really? I'm flattered. (*He has a sudden idea*) Wait! A little tache and a big arse? You know, an aggressive arse with a blue feather; not in his arse, in a pork pie hat?

Sonia's silence gives consent

(*Moving to the window*) So he was a private eye, and I thought he fancied me! Yes, there he is. (*Opening the window and looking out*) Hullo! Cooee! It's me. Remember? I blew you a kiss outside Chalk Farm station. Look, your lady is here, so there's no point in hanging around. Push off home— and well done. (*To Sonia*) He's not budging.

Sonia (*nervously, chewing a nail*) Oh, forget him.

Jay No! Standing about like that could give him athlete's foot, or piles or something. I suppose he called you from that phone box, so, when you got here, why didn't you tell the poor chap to knock off?

Sonia (*irritated*) Because he wasn't there; at least, I couldn't see him.

Jay Aha! Had to slip away for a minute, which raises an interesting point.

(*Leaning out of the window again*) I say! Could you come a bit closer? I want to whisper. Oh, all right, don't. (*Loudly*) When you're tailing someone on your own, what do you do about having a pee? No, not you, madam. So sorry! I'm talking to the gent in the pork pie hat, who is a *detective*. (*To Sonia*) He's turned his back. Looks huffy. I've noticed that before. People with those aggressive arses often lack a sense of humour.

Sonia If you've quite finished your comedy spot, is it too much to ask for an explanation?

Jay (*walking away from the window*) Darling, if I tried to explain you wouldn't understand.

Sonia You're the public relations whizz. That's your strong suit, conning the gullible into believing a pack of lies. Go on, then! Sell me the joys of Primrose Hill!

Jay (*finding it difficult*) I don't want to hurt you . . .

Sonia But it's all my fault!

Jay Irrelevant, darling. The survivor of an earthquake doesn't care which particular fault caused the disaster. He's just happy to survive.

Sonia God! I talk about our marriage. You talk about a disaster.

Jay Then we're talking about the same thing.

Sonia Oh, witty!

Jay Sorry. I do bring out the worst in me, don't I? But what marriage, Sonia? Maybe actresses shouldn't marry. I know I wanted a wife, and all I got was a frustrated career.

Sonia (*hotly*) How can you say that . . .?

Jay With sincerity. You wouldn't have a child. Why? Because of the stretch marks. Stretch marks! It isn't a partnership, it's a conflict, a competition. The more successful I become, the more you seem to resent it, compete.

Sonia So it *is* all my fault.

Jay No! Of course not. Initially, we both got together for all the wrong reasons.

Sonia Oh? And what wrong reasons prompted me to marry you?

Jay Partly the aspiring actress's inevitable insecurity, and the knowledge that my PR connections could hoist you off page three of the *Sun*, up to the dizzy heights of Hickey, Dempster and the other gossip columns.

Sonia Nothing about being in love?

Jay I don't think you're capable of love, Sonia.

Sonia What does that mean?

Jay You're too busy hating yourself.

Sonia Oh, blimey! Lead me to your couch!

Jay You'll never be able to love, until you can accept love, and you won't accept love until you've learned to love yourself.

Sonia (*leaping up*) You pompous little . . . (*She threatens to throw an ashtray at him*)

Jay (*gently restraining her by the wrist*) Sonia, no. We've hurled our last insults and heavy objects. The war is over.

Sonia (*near to tears, sitting down and lighting another cigarette*) All right, so suddenly you decide to walk out. Why?

Jay I'm starting a new life with a radical new philosophy of my own creation.

Sonia And when did this revelation hit you?

Jay Initially in the bath. I was lying in the bath one morning thinking about death.

Sonia Death!

Jay It's my age. The first thing I used to read in the morning paper was Peanuts; now it's the obituary column to see who I've survived.

Sonia You're sidetracking yourself.

Jay No. There was this old member of my club. Ninety-one he was, but bright as a button. He always lunched there and everybody loved him. Never a day passed without someone saying: "It'll be a sad day for us all when old Cecil Hobday goes." Well, he duly went. I was at the club, reading the notice announcing his death when one of his closest cronies came up and stood beside me. "Good Lord!" he said. "Old Cecil's snuffed it. I wonder what's for lunch?"

Sonia What the hell has that to do with anything?

Jay A lot. It made me realize how few people are really affected when someone dies. In fact, only one person in this world will be completely shattered by my death.

Sonia I'll buy it. Who?

Jay Me.

Sonia How could you be affected? You'd be bloody dead.

Jay But if nobody really cares whether I'm alive or dead why shouldn't I live the rest of my life exactly as I want?

Sonia Don't you always? What's new?

Jay For a start, having decided that the Public Relations man is the lowest form of human life, I shall close the office. No more scrabbling after gimmicks, no more crawling. I can't tell you what a kick I shall get from telling important clients to go stuff themselves.

Sonia And then?

Jay The joy of freedom, knowing that never again will I spend five minutes with anyone I don't choose to.

Sonia Now we're getting somewhere! You're just trotting out every middle-aged man's fantasy of becoming a bachelor again.

Jay (*equably*) Maybe a touch of that. Who doesn't occasionally hanker after a little youthful irresponsibility?

The phone rings. Sonia swiftly beats Jay to it and answers it

Sonia (*on the phone*) Hullo? Yes. Who wants him? . . . Oh, just a moment. (*Covering the mouthpiece*) Here's your chance. It's number one Arab client, Sheik Yalami, from the Mountford Hotel.

Jay How the hell did he . . .? (*He takes the phone, and talks into it*) Spencer. . . . Yes, put him through. (*To Sonia*) Miss Parfitt must have given him this number.

Sonia How comforting to learn that dear Miss Parfitt doesn't need a detective to track you down.

He waves her to silence. When he speaks, there is a subtle change in his manner; a definite hint of subservience

Jay (*on the phone*) Yes, Your Highness, I am terribly sorry not to have got
back to you, but it's been like a madhouse with half a dozen different things
... (*Hastily*) No! No! I haven't been neglecting you. I'll have the full
proposals ready for you the day after tomorrow. ... Tomorrow? Right,
tomorrow it shall be. I saw the architect and he reckons three months for
the renovation of the foyer. ... Two months? Well, I can but ask him. ...
I'll *tell* him. Right. Two months it is. Now, we do have one problem which
I'm afraid is going to mean the loss of considerable revenue. Well, once it's
officially announced that you, an Arab, have acquired the hotel the Bar
Mitzvahs are obviously out. ... (*Looking astonished*) The Bar Mitzvahs
are *in*? Your Highness, with respect, you do know what a Bar Mitzvah is?
... You do. Well, that's very ... exceedingly broad. ... Right! Right! I'll
put an ad in the *Jewish Chronicle*. See you tomorrow, at seven. Seven p.m.
it is. ... Seven *a.m.* No! No! No problem. I'll be there. Goodbye, Your
Highness. (*He hangs up, looking a little shell-shocked*) Oy ve! Maybe we
should convert the ballroom into a synagogue.

Sonia (*clapping slowly*) That was really telling him! How to get an Arab
prince to stuff himself.

Jay I said I was closing down, but not in one fell swoop. I have to eat—and
so do you.

Sonia But how will you get by after the last Bar Mitzvah has sounded?

Jay (*shrugging*) I'll ponce off some rich woman, go back to serious writing,
rob a bank. I dunno.

Sonia But how will you *live*? You've never made a bed or washed up a plate,
and the only time you cooked supper you tried to roast a boiled egg.

Jay There's always the Moti Mahal.

Sonia looks bank

Indian restaurant across the street. They have fourteen wallpapers and
forty curries. Or is it forty wallpapers and fourteen curries?

Sonia (*moving towards the bed*) Pathetic! A round bed at your age!

Jay A lifetime in oblong ones has got me nowhere, so what the hell?

Sonia It has to be someone else. Come on. Is it?

Jay (*after a pause*) All right—yes.

Sonia (*almost relieved*) So it is another woman.

Jay No.

Sonia What! What? It's a *man*?

Jay Well, yes. It's me.

Sonia stares at him

I have fallen in love with me.

Sonia I can't believe I'm hearing this.

Jay Why should you? As I said, you don't love you. I'm different. I've
learned how great it is to be me, to live with me. I can honestly say I'm one
of the best adjusted couples I know.

Sonia If you could listen to yourself!

Jay Oh, I do. I've just discovered the joy of talking to myself, agreeing with everything I say. Never a cross word. The perception, the wit, the charm! You think I'm crazy, don't you?

Sonia I know you are.

Jay No. A little over excited maybe, but why not? I'm re-born, you see. This isn't the sixteen thousand three hundred and thirty-first day of a routinely miserable existence. It is the first, joyous day of a brand new life.

Sonia Happy birthday!

Jay Thank you.

Sonia You know what your trouble really is?

Jay Oh, dear! Here come the *Reader's Digest* snippets on the male menopause.

Sonia (*it's true*) No ... I ... well, actually ...

Jay Wrong tack, darling. The menopausal subject dreads the future. I don't. I look forward to it. He is haunted by the spectre of old age; worried days, sleepless nights. Will I get it up? Will it stay up if I do get it up?

Sonia Now it begins to sound depressingly like you.

Jay *Touché!* But in recent weeks, neither my ego nor anything else has been uplifted by you hopping straight from my bed on to movie mogul Carlo Cassini's casting couch in Cavendish Cloisters. I say! What a lot of words starting with C—and I just thought of another.

Sonia (*clearly shaken*) Finally it comes. So that's what this is all about. How long have you known?

Jay More or less from the off—or should it be on?

Sonia And you said nothing.

Jay What did you want me to say: "Evening, darling. How many orgasms this afternoon?"

Sonia But you must have wanted to say something?

Jay Yes, "Evening, darling. How many orgasms this afternoon?"

Sonia But not a word ...

Jay Making a scene wouldn't have stopped you; just ensured you were more careful.

Sonia (*awkwardly*) About Carlo ...

Jay No need to fill me in on Carlo. I checked. One of the best lays of ancient Rome.

Sonia What do you intend to do?

Jay Don't worry. I'm not going to murder him. I can safely leave that to the film critics. Any movie entitled *Emanuelle And The Devil's Dyke* has to be slaughtered.

Sonia (*floundering*) It ... isn't ... like what you think it is; him and me.

Jay Surprise me.

Sonia I admit getting into his film is terribly important to me. It's my big chance, perhaps my only chance with the business in the state it's in. As to the—other side. Carlo not only believes in me as an actress, he's very much in love with me.

Jay You're not being a teensy bit gullible?

Sonia (*defiantly*) If I were free he'd marry me.

Jay Then he may have to put his money where his mouth is sooner than he thinks. Do you have a contract?

Sonia Not yet, because ...
Jay Take my advice and get one, fast.
Sonia The thing is, I may not play the part he'd earmarked for me. I may play something different.
Jay Don't tell me you're the dyke?

She chews her nails

Nails!
Sonia There's something you don't know. Fiona Sutton has fallen out.
Jay Of what?
Sonia The film. She's asking too much money. She was playing Emanuelle.
Jay Oh? (*Getting the message*) You? You've got the lead?

She nods

Fantastic! I can see the headlines when I write my piece for the *Sunday People*. "I was married to Emanuelle the sixty-ninth."
Sonia *Was* married?
Jay I'm assuming we'll be cosily divorced by then. You might even be Mrs Cassini ...
Sonia Look, Jay, this whole thing in Cavendish Cloisters ...
Jay Thing? That's not a very nice way to talk about old Carlo. He's quite pretty—except for the ears.
Sonia (*sidetracked*) Ears?
Jay You haven't noticed? No, you probably don't walk behind him very often. (*Pushing his own ears forward*) Amazing—but handy for gliding out of bedroom windows in a hurry.
Sonia Shut up! Shut up!
Jay I apologize. That was uncalled for and if the rest of him stands out half as ...
Sonia Oh, for God's sake! I'm trying to say I'm not in love with him and it probably won't last.
Jay I see. Get the film, make it, then ditch him. Meanwhile, you'd like me to hang around as a safety net.
Sonia I didn't mean that.
Jay Funny thing about safety nets. People don't appreciate their importance until suddenly they're not there any more.
Sonia (*with a hint of panic*) I know I'm impossible, a mess, but I do need you.
Jay Well you've got a bloody odd way of showing it.
Sonia I don't know what it is with me ...
Jay I told you—insecurity, the compulsion to prove yourself irresistible to all men. (*Wearily*) I understand it but, suddenly, I can't live with it.
Sonia I realize things have been lousy, but, in a funny way, we're good for each other. You provide stability and I provide a—a—sort of stimulus, spur ...
Jay "Creative conflict" they call it, don't they? Trouble is I'm a pacifist at heart.
Sonia Before we married you were considered unimaginative and old-

fashioned. You may despise what you do, but now you're one of the most successful PR men in London.

Jay Dubious compliment—like saying someone is a first-class flasher. (*Looking at his watch*) Hey, look at the time. Won't old Carlo be waiting?

Sonia (*embarrassed*) Yes. We're having dinner but I needn't ... I wouldn't go if you didn't want me to.

Jay I've nothing to offer you, except a tin of ravioli.

Sonia You silly idiot! What are you doing in this dump with tins of ravioli? Come home. (*She pulls him towards her and kisses him hard*)

Initially he resists and then we see his defences crumbling as her undoubted physical attraction gets to him. She makes a move towards the bed. With an obvious effort, he regains his determination and wrenches himself free

Jay No, Sonia, please. Don't make this more difficult than it is.

Sonia You'll come back. You know you want to. You could never live alone.

Jay I have to try. I have to, or I'll shrivel up and die. I'm sorry, really sorry.

Sonia stifles a sob, turns away and runs for the nearest shelter, which is the bathroom

She enters the bathroom, slamming the door behind her

Jay draws a deep breath. He looks drained. The front door, which is ajar, slowly opens

Darlene enters, clad as before, in a shirt

Darlene I'm going out after some. If you want any I can get it, or you can have a bit of mine.

Jay This sounds a fascinating proposition. A bit of your what?

Darlene Bread. Or I'll buy you some if you like.

Jay Don't bother ...

Darlene No bother. I have to go out now, anyway.

Jay Right away?

Darlene Yes.

Jay Dressed like that?

Darlene The shop's only at the corner.

Jay That should make the baker's dough rise!

Jay gives her a smile which is not returned. She is not the smiling type

Darlene It's not a bakery. It's a little grocers', run by some Pakis. What sort of bread?

Jay Wholemeal, please, and sliced, of course. (*Taking a pound note from his wallet, and proffering it*) Here.

Darlene That's all right.

Jay (*pressing the money on her*) I insist. My mother taught me never to accept bread from strange girls.

Darlene Why?

Jay Never mind. We never did introduce ourselves. I'm Jay. (*He proffers his hand*)

Darlene (*taking his hand*) Darlene.

Sonia enters from the bathroom. Seeing Jay and Darlene holding hands she could be forgiven if she mishears "Darlene" for "darling"

Jay Darlene.

Darlene sees Sonia, sneezes, then exits through the front door

Jay closes the door, and turns to face Sonia, with a social smile

Sonia And who, precisely, is that?

Jay (*promptly*) The Princess Helga von und zu Unterschlitzen from the House of Hesse, but she rarely uses the title. She models men's shirts. That was one of them.

Sonia Where did you dig that up?

Jay Garden Party at Buckingham Palace. Our eyes met across a crowded lawn, while the band of Grenadiers played *Colonel Bogey*. (*Humming the tune*) Tum-tum-tee-tum-tum-tum-tum-tee. I offered her a winkle and that was it.

Sonia And how old is she, may I ask?

Jay Forty-eight. Never think so, would you?

A ring on the front door certainly saves Jay from a physical assault. Jay opens the door

Darlene stands outside

Princess! That was quick!

Darlene It's a ropey little shop. They might not have wholemeal.

Jay Never mind.

Darlene What would you say to a Hovis?

Jay I'd say: "Hullo, Hovis. Come in for a bite." Ha! Ha!

She turns away, still unsmiling

You should put on your wellies. Some idiot has broken a milk bottle on the front steps.

Darlene Yes, me. I'll give it to you later.

Darlene exits

Jay (*closing the door*) There! Isn't that exciting? She's going to give it to me later.

Sonia You turd! You devious, lying, two-faced little turd! You couldn't come into the open, could you? Oh, no! You had to play the faithful, hard-done-by husband. God, you repel me!

Jay Yes, you have made that pretty clear lately.

Sonia You're a moral and physical coward. A flop in life and a flop in bed.

Jay (*raising a hand*) Please, ma'am. You only partially succeeded in castrating me. At lunchtime today a girl and I split a bottle of champagne to celebrate the re-born me. One thing led to another and I conclusively proved that everything is fine in that area. Twice. (*Proudly*) *Very nearly* three times.

Sonia I'm glad you've left me and when you're ditched by this over-sexed little tramp don't come crawling back. I don't want you. You're a nothing, a nobody; a fourth-rate man with a third-rate mind and a secondhand wit—and your breath smells.

Jay (*mildly*) Otherwise no complaints?

Enraged, Sonia swipes him hard with her handbag and exits through the front door, leaving it open

Jay, looking thoughtful, closes the front door and then moves straight to the phone. He looks up a number from a diary kept in his hip pocket and taps it out

(*On the phone*) *Pronto? Signor Carlo Cassini per piacere. . . . Ah! Carlo! Ciaou!* (*It has sounded good, but this is the limit of his Italian*) This is Jay Spencer here. . . . Jay Spencer. . . . *Spencer*! The chap whose wife you've been sc . . . . That's it! No, wait! Non panico, Carlo. Sonia and I have just had a *wonderful* talk about you—two adult human beings discussing their problems in a most civilized manner. (*Rubbing his arm where she hit him*) We have agreed to part as friends. I won't say it doesn't hurt but I hope I'm man enough sincerely to wish you both a long and productive life together, in films and family-wise, with hordes of little . . . hullo? . . . Carlo? Are you there? . . . Oh, you are! You sound kind of—well, I expect you're all choked up, like me. So let's leave it there and all I can do is wish you the best of Brit . . . the best of luck. (*He hangs up. He moves away, quietly humming "Arrivaderci Roma" to himself. He eyes the bed, then picks up the pocket recorder from the dining-table, and talks into it*) Miss Parfitt, check with Bill Boynton at London Electricity re circular electric blankets. Do they exist? If they do, I want one, free, and in return, I'll get him a mention in one of the columns.

The doorbell rings and Jay goes and opens the front door

Darlene is revealed, carrying a paper bag containing a loaf

Princess!

Darlene (*entering*) Why do you call me that?

Jay Shan't tell you. Too ashamed.

Darlene The Pakis didn't have any Hovis. Only one of those Jewish loaves, it's got seeds on top. I think they're seeds.

Jay So long as they're not weevils. (*Taking the loaf*) They're not. Thanks.

Darlene (*handing him his change*) It isn't sliced. They hadn't any sliced.

Jay Who cares? I'll gouge out great chunks with my fingers. You can behave like a pig when you live on your own.

Darlene (*looking at the bed*) I've never slept in a round bed.

Jay Any time you feel like a nap, pop in. That's a free offer, not a rude thing.

Darlene I won't be here.

Jay Sorry to hear that. Obliging neighbours are a rarity these days. Going away?

Darlene (*hesitantly*) Yes. (*Changing tack*) I ran into your friend in the street.

Jay Friend? Oh, that was no friend. That was my wife.

Darlene She called me a disgusting word.

Jay Tart, whore, hooker, something original like that?

Darlene No.

Jay Oh! (*He gives a suppressed laugh*) She didn't, did she? She did! I'm afraid she's addicted to foul language. Her father was a sergeant major.

Darlene Is she a bit mad?

Jay No, she's an actress; or, yes, she's an actress.

Darlene She's got cold eyes.

Jay (*nodding*) Which were my downfall.

Darlene How?

Jay On a beach in Cannes during the Film Festival. There was this strange girl looking right at me, with an intense, burning stare.

Darlene Trying to pull you.

Jay Not at all. She was admiring her own reflection in my dark glasses. Should have been a warning.

Darlene Are you and she . . .?

Jay Divorcing, I hope.

Darlene You hope?

Jay Contrary creatures, you women. You'll take a man for granted for years; then, if it looks as if you're losing him, he suddenly becomes the most desirable object in the world. Would you like a cup of tea?

Darlene I don't mind.

Jay Good. My first party. No dainty cakes, I'm afraid.

He exits to the kitchen, carrying the loaf

Darlene She's younger than you, isn't she?

Jay (*off*) Kind of you to put that as a question. Yes.

He comes out of the kitchen, carrying a box, which should contain teabags

Darlene Is that why it didn't work?

Jay No. I could cite you twenty ideally matched couples age-wise, whose marriages have sunk without trace. I hope you don't mind teabags. (*Opening the box, which is empty*) Don't answer that. There aren't any. You don't fancy a cup of hot water? No, why should you? Tell you what, Princess, I have a better idea.

Darlene I wish you wouldn't call me Princess.

Jay What shall I call you then?

Darlene What's wrong with Darlene?

Jay Everything. It's quite the nastiest name I ever heard. Who thought it up?

Jay exits to the kitchen

Darlene My dad.

Jay (*off*) He should be shot.

Darlene He's dead.

Jay enters from the kitchen, carrying a bottle of champagne

Jay Sorry.

Darlene (*shrugging*) I never knew him. He dropped dead just after I was born.

Jay Struck down for calling you Darlene. Have to find something else. For the moment we'll settle for darling. So, darling, you and I will christen the flat with this. Non vintage, but it's nice and cold. (*He starts to open the bottle*)

Darlene (*suddenly going towards the door*) Is that my phone? (*She listens at the door, looks disappointed then comes back*)

Jay Expecting a call?

Darlene (*depressed*) Not really. (*Sighing*) No.

Jay gets the cork out, which comes out without a pop

Jay No pop. May be flat. (*He tilts the bottle. Nothing comes out. He examines the bottle closely*) It's frozen solid. My fridge has turned itself into a freezer. (*He raises the bottle, and pretends to drink*) Glug-glug-glug . . .

Darlene does not smile at any of this. Jay, probably deciding that she is a bore, steals a look at his watch

Well, that seems to end our little orgy.

Darlene does not take the hint. She heaves a dramatic sigh

I may be quite wrong, but I have an idea you're not too happy about something.

Darlene nods and sighs again

I was right! And you're aching to tell me all about it.

Darlene (*she is*) No.

Jay (*swiftly*) Good. It's better left unsaid.

Darlene Why?

Jay Keep it bottled up like that champagne. What you don't know doesn't make you unhappy.

Darlene But I *do* know. And I *am* unhappy.

Jay But I don't. Half the people staying happy is better than all the people being miserable. Right?

Darlene tries to work this out, mouthing what he has said

I say, is that really the time?

Darlene (*not taking any hint*) Are you unhappy?

Jay Me? No.

Darlene I bet you are, but you're bottling it up like you said.

Jay No. I'm definitely not a candidate for the gas oven—not that the oven is any use these days.

Darlene Eh?

Jay You can't kill yourself with North Sea Gas.

Darlene (*startled*) You can't?

Jay So I'm told.

Darlene But—why not?

Jay (*shrugging*) Perhaps it's filtered pure coming up through all that filthy, oily water.

Darlene No-one ever told me.

Jay Oh course, another way is to shut the windows, turn on the gas tap, wait a few minutes then strike a match.. You get one hell of an explosion.

Darlene But that might kill other people.

Jay Certainly! Blows a house to smithereens.

Darlene That's no good, then.

Jay (*smiling*) You're not thinking of committing suicide, are you?

Darlene Yes.

Jay Oh.

Darlene I am.

Jay When?

Darlene Now, after tea.

Jay Wait! That reminds me. I do have some coffee—if you can stand instant.

Darlene You are funny.

Jay Ha-ha, or peculiar?

Darlene Peculiar. I said I was going to kill myself.

Jay Yes.

Darlene You just said: "Oh".

Jay Oh, did I?

Darlene Yes.

Jay Ah.

Darlene Then talked about coffee.

Jay Only just remembered I had some. Did you say yes, or no?

Darlene I said I was going to kill myself, yes.

Jay I meant about the coffee. Yes or no?

Darlene No. Don't you want to know why?

Jay Why you don't want coffee?

Darlene No! Why I'm going to kill myself.

Jay Actually—no; not very much, thanks all the same.

Darlene You'll just let me go ahead and do it?

Jay Not in here, please.

Darlene (*crossly*) Of course I won't do it in here!

Jay Good girl.

Darlene But if I go away to do it, you wouldn't try and stop me?

Jay No. Who am I to interfere?

Darlene But anyone would try and stop a person.

Jay Why?

Darlene Well, they ... they would.

Jay Don't see it. If you want to kill yourself why should I poke my nose in?

Darlene You're a weirdo.

Jay You want to end it all?

Darlene Yes.

Jay Your mind is irretrievably made up?

Darlene Yes.

Jay It isn't because of me, anything I've done?

Darlene Course it isn't. I don't know you.

Jay And I don't know you.

Darlene What's that to do with it?

Jay So it's your business, not mine and, as from today, I'm resolved only to mind my own business.

Darlene You really are creepy.

Jay Just logical. Why should I care whether you continue to exist when, ten minutes ago, I didn't know you even existed?

Darlene You know now.

Jay Must I don the mantle of father-protector because you bought me a seedy old loaf?

Darlene You could behave like a normal person.

Jay Why don't you try that? If you were really serious you'd shut yourself away and gollop some pills.

Darlene (*triumphantly producing two bottles of pills*) I've got the pills—aspirin and Ominol; enough to kill an army.

Jay Could you spare me one aspirin? You've given me a headache. (*He stretches out a hand*)

Darlene (*hastily pulling the bottles out of his reach*) No. I once read a book. It said that suicide was a cry for help.

Jay No, it didn't.

Darlene It did! I ...

Jay It almost certainly said that people who talk about committing suicide are really crying: "Help! Stop me!" Nine times out of ten they have no intention of doing it. It's merely a way of insuring that some kind-hearted fool has to listen to their tedious sob story.

Darlene You've very hard, aren't you?

Jay Not yet, darling, but, hopefully, my new shell is thickening by the hour.

Darlene (*rising and going to the front door*) Don't strike any matches.

Jay Bluff.

Darlene Wait and see.

Jay Why blow up your poor flat?

Darlene It isn't mine. I only borrowed it.

Jay All the more reason to use those lovely lethal pills!

Darlene I'd hate to be married to you.

Jay You are not alone.

Darlene You have a gruesome mind.

Jay You have gorgeous tits.

Darlene exits, slamming the front door

Well, at least she didn't call you a dirty old man.

The flap of the letter-box in the front door opens with quite a bang

Darlene (*through the letter-box*) And I think you're a dirty old man.

The flap closes with a bang

Jay "I *think* you're a dirty old man." Not "You *are* a dirty old man." Was there an element of doubt there? (*He mounts the rostrum and sits on the bed. Something on the wooden surround of the alcove catches his eye. He looks closely at it, then straightens up, shaking his head*) Too much!

The doorbell rings

(*Mimicking Darlene*) You *are* a dirty old man. (*He opens the front door*)

Rose stands outside. Her hair may be greying and is conservatively neat. Her figure is trim and discreet. She is inclined towards a bright smile, in contrast to her dress, which, although of reasonable quality, is drab and colourless. She carries a useful handbag

Jay looks at her blankly, clearly not knowing who she is

(*Politely*) Good-afternoon?

Rose Jason!

Jay (*giving a slight start, he looks closer then takes a step backwards*) Rose? Rose!

Rose May I come in?

Rose enters and looks round the room, an action which, for some reasons, moves her deeply. She puts a hand to her mouth

Oh, Jason!

Jay (*incredulously*) I can't believe this. I was thinking of you at that moment; that precise moment.

Rose Jason, you came back to our first little home.

Jay Moved in today. Rose, how ...?

Rose (*cutting in*) Why? Why did you come here?

Jay Pure chance. I was looking for somewhere to plonk myself, happened to pass the house and saw a board up.

Rose And you snapped it up.

Jay It appealed to my sense of the absurd. I mean, twenty years!

Rose You don't believe in Providence bringing people together?

Jay No. So how come you're here? How could you possibly know?

Rose Please, my dear, I will explain but give me a moment——

Jay OK. Meanwhile, here's something to give you a giggle. (*Beckoning her to follow him to the alcove surround*) Look there.

Rose looks and gasps

Rose "Jason", "Rose" — our names! I remember us carving them!

Jay Little vandals!

Rose Yes, I felt terribly wicked. But you said: "What the heck? The flat is ours for ..."

Jay Forty years. We were not only young vandals, we were over optimistic young vandals. I spotted it one second before you knocked on the door. Eerie.

Rose I remember the first time you brought me here as if it was yesterday.

Jay So do I.

Rose (*touched*) Really?

Jay You wore red pants and a white polo neck. You walked through that door, stopped and looked around. You looked very pretty and very, very young.

Rose (*sadly*) I was.

Jay You said: "Yes, this is it." Then you sat on an upturned sugar box there, turned and looked at me in a way which sent a warm glow right through me. Pure love. Sad.

Rose Sad?

Jay Sad because it never happens again, not like that. First love—innocent, unquestioning, uncomplicated, so confident of its durability. Foolish? Maybe, but very precious while it lasts. (*Shaking off the nostalgia*) That's quite enough of that!

Rose (*stretching out and squeezing one of his hands*) Dear Jason, you look tired and much, much older.

Jay (*with a slight edge*) And you look ... (*controlling himself*) fine. The figure's great and I like the—(*searching for the right word*)—the—um ...

Rose Frock?

Jay Frock! Yes. That really is a frock.

Rose It's as old as the hills.

Jay An old favourite. I guessed. Where are you living, Rose?

Rose Not far away. Neasden.

Jay Neasden! I have always liked the sound of Neasden. (*Indicating the window*) You can see it from that window with binoculars.

There is an awkward pause

Rose (*moving away to look out of the window*) The old street looks much the ... oh no! (*Pointing*) That restaurant. The Moti Mahal!

Jay Still there. Remember the plump Indian kid you force-fed with Maltesers?

Rose Abdul!

Jay Abdul! Your memory. He's now a plump Indian man of about thirty-two. The old chap died.

Rose They were a sweet little family, most civilized.

Jay Why not? This is North West Three, not the North West Frontier.

Rose You know what I mean—sweet. I wonder if Abdul remembers us?

Jay I doubt it. He swears he does, but the Bengalis are renowned for their tact.

Rose Wait a sec! One bindaloo hot and mild korma!

Jay (*indicating the phone*) You want to order? They do take-aways.

Rose No. You can't have forgotten that. *Our* order. And there was that gorgeous sambo.

Jay Sambo? A chap called *Sambo*, in an Indian Restaurant?

Rose No! Sambo—the hot gravy which goes with potato pancake things!

Jay Dosai with sam*bar*.

Rose Sam*ba* was it?

Jay S-A-M-B-A-R and, by the way it's vin with a v not bin and it's pronounced vind*ah*loo.

There is an awkward silence

Rose I haven't had it since.

Jay A curry you mean?

Rose Yes. It disagrees with George. He perspires. (*She walks around the room*)

Jay How—disagreeable. But where are my manners? (*Going to the drinks*) Can I offer you something? Bit limited I'm afraid. I have hot water, black coffee, frozen champagne, gin, whisky and some rather rye bread ...

Rose Nothing, my dear, thank you. It's going to be super here, but what a mess! (*She tidies a couple of things, taking out a tissue and doing a little dusting*) Thick with dust.

Jay (*slightly edgy*) Don't worry ...

Rose I can see you need taking in hand.

Jay I will be. I have a girl ...

Rose (*looking up*) A girl?

Jay To come in and clean. It's all organized. Rose, please, you're making me fidgety.

Rose And you're obviously itching to know how I found you and what I'm doing here.

Jay Since I only moved in an hour ago and haven't seen or talked to you for decades—yes, you could say I was a trifle itchy.

Rose You're going to be furious.

Jay I've given up fury, disagrees with me, makes me perspire.

Rose The truth is we've been looking rather drab and shabby and decided we had to do something about it.

Jay (*gallantly*) And you've triumphed. The whole *ensemble*, completed by that frock ...

Rose No, you old silly! I'm talking about my flat! It hadn't been decorated for ages. Pennies are pretty short since inflation.

Jay Sorry to hear that.

Rose (*ever cheerful*) We manage; but we had to look for a reasonable little man to do the job, and I suddenly remembered—Mr Murphy!

Jay What!

Rose Yes, *our* sweet Mr Murphy.

Jay *My* sweet Mr Murphy, who should be working here but suddenly stopped because his sister in Cork was taken bad with her legs. You, I assume, are the Cork-legged sister?

Rose (*guiltily*) Perhaps I am! But it was only a quick job and, in a couple of days, he has worked marvels in the flat, marvels.

Jay Marvellous.

Rose He looks much, much older, too.

Jay (*with a hint of asperity*) He *is* older. He's entitled.

Rose Matured, of course. Quite widely read, you know. Talks endlessly on any subject.

Jay I know. Anything rather than get down to work.

Rose We got on like a house on fire. (*She gives a tinkling laugh*) He even invited me to dinner! (*Confidentially*) His wife died.

Jay He probably bored her to death.

Rose Anyway, it was amazing to find him again after all these years. When we first knew him he was really only a boy. He built up quite a business, but now ...

Jay Yes, Rose, I know. *I* found him again before you did, remember?

Rose Anyway, as I said, we got chatting over endless mugs of tea. (*Winking*) They like you to have a chat with them, don't they? One thing led to another and he let slip about you buying this place. I put two and two together and realized you must be leaving that Sonia.

Jay Bloody Murphy! He can whistle for his bill.

Rose You are furious.

Jay No. Not with you anyway.

Rose (*nervously*) Then you are pleased to see me?

Jay (*straightfaced*) Pleased is not the word.

Rose (*missing any arrow*) Thank goodness! I know I should have written or phoned. In fact, I did call your office but you were out, and I didn't try again because, frankly, I was terrified you might refuse to meet.

Jay (*frowning*) No-one at the office told me . . .

Rose I didn't say who I was. I chatted with a very pleasant sounding woman . . .

Jay Miss Parfitt, my secretary.

Rose She sounds jolly nice.

Jay Jolly is the word; definite case for an acute hearty attack.

Rose How dreadful. Something congenital?

Jay No, that was a jo——forget it. Talking of health, very remiss of me. Apart from the perspiration problems, how is old Jack?

Rose (*blankly*) Jack?

Jay (*laughing*) You married him, Rose! The man who stole you from me.

Rose You mean George.

Jay George! You're right! Didn't I say George? Anyway, how is he? Fighting fit?

Rose (*sadly*) Far from it. We must have a long talk about that.

Jay (*glancing at his watch*) A very long talk?

Rose Yes, but not just now. I want to hear all about you first. How *are* you, Jason?

Jay Great; never better.

Rose No, really?

Jay Really. A little tired and looking much, much older, but fine. Why?

Rose You've been through hell, haven't you?

Jay I wouldn't say that.

Rose You wouldn't. You're too good, but one hears things, you know.

Jay Does one? From whom? What about?

Rose (*embarrassed*) From people—about Sonia.

Jay You mean strangers stop you in the street and say: "You're the first Mrs Spencer, aren't you? Did you know that poor old Jay is going through hell with the current Mrs Spencer?"

Rose Nancy Latimer is one of the few people who has kept friendly with both of us.

Jay Not for much longer. What has she been saying?

Rose (*after a pause*) Jason, one of the things I've learned, late in life, is that sometimes one should tell the truth, even if it hurts.

Jay I'd say always, but carry on.

Rose (*blurting it out*) To be blunt Sonia has been — well — been sleeping around all over London.

Jay And a few times in Hemel Hempstead, but I think that one is over now.

Rose You know!

Jay Contrary to popular belief, the husband isn't always the last to know.

Rose And you stand for it?

Jay Some people take a long time to grow up. Sonia is one of them.

Rose But, Jason, she is making you a laughing stock.

Jay (*laughing incredulously*) You are priceless!

Rose (*puzzled*) Am I?

Jay If some friend or acquaintance tells me I'm a laughing stock, I might take heed. But coming from you, Rose! Damn it, you started the fashion in laughing stocks. You walked out on me.

Rose Yes, you're right. You may not believe me, but I have never forgiven myself for what I did to you. Not a day has passed when I have not agonized about it.

Jay Not a day — in all those years?

Rose (*nodding*) We have both lived with an abiding sense of guilt.

Jay Both? You mean old Geoff has agonized, too?

Rose George. Yes, more than you could imagine. Of course, your wonderful lack of bitterness and recrimination made us feel worse.

Jay If it would have made you feel better I'd have charged round and thumped him on the nose.

Rose You? Never! I only started to find peace of mind when you married Janet and achieved the happiness you deserve. Then that ghastly accident. I can only tell you — my world crumbled.

Jay *Your* world? (*Sarcastically*) I'm sorry to hear that!

Rose It was shattering. You did get our letter of condolence?

Jay Um — yes. I'm sure I did. Yes. I hope I replied?

Rose No, but I quite understood.

Jay That was extremely ill-mannered of me. Apologize to old Jim, too.

Rose George. (*Managing a laugh*) Do try and get his name right!

Jay Damn! George! *George!* I've always had a hang-up about his name — Freudian perhaps. I can't remember what he looks like, either. If he marched into this room now I wouldn't know him.

Rose He looks simply dreadful since his illness. You wouldn't know him.

Jay That's what I said . . . Oh, you mean I wouldn't know him even if I would know him . . . Illness?

Rose I'll tell you about that later.

Jay Later. (*Giving another look at his watch*) I'll look forward to that. Yes.

Rose Then when I heard you'd married Sonia I was over the moon. According to everyone she was attractive and intelligent. I'm so terribly sorry it has gone wrong.

Jay That's life.

Rose It doesn't have to be. This is why I summoned up the courage to come, because I only survived owing to a wonderful piece of luck.

Jay The pools?

Rose (*in a low voice*) Jesus.

Jay Who?
Rose Jesus Christ. I found Him.
Jay (*somewhat bemused*) I didn't know he'd ... You found him? Where?

*Rose is by no means mad but when riding this particular hobby-horse she is
definitely transported*

Rose He was waiting for me, Jason, with arms out-stretched. He has given
me the strength to live with my sins, to face up to all my problems—and
I've had a few! He has given me His forgiveness. He has given me faith.
Jay (*slightly uncomfortable*) That's great. Congratulations.
Rose Above all, He has taught me to laugh again. I'd forgotten how, but now
I laugh all the time, because there is renewed joy in my heart. (*She laughs*)
Coming here this afternoon on the tube I suddenly burst out laughing and
everyone looked at me so strangely!
Jay Ye-es, they would.
Rose And He can do the same for you.
Jay I don't actually use the tube much.
Rose And, of course, He it was who guided me here.
Jay It wasn't really Mr Murphy, then?
Rose Mr Murphy was just His chosen envoy.
Jay I say! Does old Murphy know that?
Rose No.
Jay You must tell him. He'll be tickled pink.
Rose I want you to join Him, Jason, as a partner.
Jay (*startled*) Mr Murphy?
Rose Jesus.
Jay Oh!
Rose You can't imagine what marvels He has worked for me.
Jay Mr Murphy?
Rose No, *Jesus*, Jason. Can we forget Mr Murphy for a moment?
Jay Yes. Very sorry. You said that he worked marvels in your flat and I got a
bit confused. (*Assuming a serious interest*) So you say that old ... that Jesus
has worked marvels, too?
Rose Yes. Oh, yes! I have no call on your everyday life, but let me be the
guide to the happiness of your soul.

The doorbell rings. Relieved, Jay opens the front door

Darlene, dressed as before but with even less buttons done up, stands outside

Darlene Have you got a tin-opener? (*Making a stabbing movement*) One of
those with a sharp end?
Jay (*horrified*) No! Don't attempt it with a tin-opener! You'll never make it.
(*Lowering his voice*) The pills—much tidier.
Darlene (*crossly*) I'm heating some baked beans and my opener's broke.
Jay (*relieved*) Sorry I can't help.

Darlene shrugs and turns away

Darling ... (*Drawing closer; lowering his voice*) Does this mean we've
abandoned the ... (*making a throat-slitting noise*) business?

Darlene No. I'm thinking about it.

Darlene exits

Jay closes the door and returns to Rose, evidently prepared to ignore the incident

Jay Now, where were we?

Rose Who on earth is that quaint little thing?

Jay No idea.

Rose Jason! You called her "darling".

Jay No—Darlene. That's what she's called—Darlene.

Rose What a pretty name!

Jay Isn't it?

Rose Who is she?

Jay I told you, I don't know.

Rose You know her well enough to call her Darlene!

Jay Rose, you're sounding like a wife again! She's Darlene something, who lives across the hall with no tin-opener, bread knife or razor, and, apparently, with a somewhat limited wardrobe.

Rose Yes! Does she always walk about in that curious attire?

Jay She always has for the hour I've lived here. Yes.

Rose Extraordinary! Wait a minute! She must be the girl Mr Murphy mentioned, who stood on that landing, sobbing, with a bicycle pump in her hand.

Jay Sounds like her.

Rose But why a bicycle pump?

Jay Wanted to blow herself up.

Rose I'm serious.

Jay You think I'm not?

Rose Apparently she was there for practically the whole of one morning that Mr Murphy was here.

Jay Which helps to explain how little work he got done.

Rose What was it you were so anxious for her not to open with a tin-opener?

Jay I'd rather not say—confidential stuff.

Rose Oh, I see! Jason, I might think she was a bit on the young side, but if she is your—you know—I wouldn't mind.

Jay Of course you wouldn't. It's none of your business is it?

Rose (*hastily*) All I meant is that you're a normal man with normal healthy appetites . . .

Jason winces

. . . so I'd quite understand.

Jay Thank you very much.

Rose (*confidentially*) *He* would understand, too.

Jay Mr Murphy?

Rose No, Jason. You seem to have something of an obsession about Mr Murphy.

Jay *I* do. You keep bringing him up.

Rose Of course I didn't mean Mr Murphy. Obviously you couldn't care less what Mr Murphy thought. (*Almost angrily*) I'm talking of Our Lord, Jason, who understands all. (*Chuckling*) One of the tiny tots in my club wrote a hymn on that very theme. "Glory to our groovy God!" (*Laughing*) Isn't that adorable?

Jay Lovely! So you run a club?

Rose For deprived children.

Jay Rewarding work.

Rose Tremendous. Uplifting. (*Changing the subject*) Before that child came in we were talking about my offer of help.

Jay Yes, and I'm extremely touched. I won't deny there have been times when I've felt I was a loser. It's easy to feel sorry for yourself and, starting with our break up, I do seem to have taken my fair share of knocks.

Rose You have. You have.

Jay But that's all over now. Look, are you sure you wouldn't like a scotch or something before you go? (*He pours himself a drink*)

Rose No, thank you. I never touch alcohol.

Jay You don't? I seem to remember you as the one sherry a night girl.

Rose The one sherry a night girl became an alcoholic.

Jay (*stunned*) You did? How? Why?

Rose You.

Jay Me?

Rose Because of what I did to you.

Jay My God! I do have a lot to answer for.

Rose It was my conscience, trying to bury it. Such guilt. I was lucky, George stood by me and when all was nearly lost, He pulled me from the pit.

Jay (*confidently*) George.

Rose No, Jesus.

Jay snaps his fingers angrily

That is when I found my faith. A year ago. I haven't touched alcohol since and never will again. I have no need of it. I have Him beside me.

Jay Geo . . . Jes . . . (*giving up*) Well, that's tremendous. I envy that kind of faith.

Rose You can find faith, too, Jason.

Jay I have, but I doubt if you'd approve of it.

Rose Oh, I'm sure I shall!?

Jay The basic tenets of my new philosophy are to forget the past, never worry about the future, to concentrate on self-approval, and not give a damn what anyone else thinks of me.

Rose (*indulgently*) Dear Jason! That just wouldn't work! Life can't be a series of detached acts. Everything one does has a direct effect on other people.

Jay But don't worry about it and don't feel guilty about anything. Guilt and worry are wasted emotions. Look at you, Rose. You break up our marriage, lead the life you have chosen, then spend eighteen years agonizing about it. What has that achieved, other than turning you into an alcoholic?

Rose One can't blot out the past. It's there.

Jay It isn't. It's gone! You're not living at all if you keep looking over your shoulder. It's today that counts. Live for now.

There is a brief, very loud explosion from somewhere beyond the front door

Rose Ah! What was that?

Jay She's blown herself up. (*Hurrying to the front door*) I should have let her have that tin-opener. You'd better stay here. This could be a messy business.

Rose (*joining him*) I was a nurse, Jason!

Jay opens the front door

Darlene staggers into the room. Her face and shirt are spattered with red, which we assume to be blood. Her eyes are closed, she is yelling like a hurt child

Darlene Can't see ... (*Her legs give way*)

Jay catches her and lifts her up. Rose goes to the rostrum

Jay (*carrying Darlene to the rostrum*) Take off the sheet. It's my only one.

Rose Augh! Bother your sheet. (*She literally seizes Darlene and lays her on the bed*) Hot water. Sponge.

Jay I don't have a sponge.

Rose Anything to scrub her up. (*She is now a nurse, capable of barking sharp orders*)

Jay exits to the kitchen

Darlene thrashes about, moaning

(*Restraining her*) It's all right, dear, lie still.

Darlene Blind ... I'm blinded.

Rose bends to examine the eyes

Jay enters from the kitchen, carrying a dishcloth

Jay Shouldn't I call a doctor? It looks pretty bad.

Rose I don't think it's as bad as it seems.

Rose examines Darlene's thighs, suddenly straightens up and pushes Jay off the rostrum

Close the curtains.

Jay (*closing the curtains using the remote control*) Is she cut badly?

Rose's head appears in the gap where the curtains meet

Rose Knickers!

Jay (*huffily*) All right! All right! I was thinking of her, not my sheet.

Rose She isn't wearing any knickers.

Jay Don't look at me! I told you, I hardly know the girl.

Rose Get her some.

Jay Where the hell would I find knickers? I'm not a transvestite ...

Rose Underpants, then; something to make her decent. (*She withdraws*)

He goes and opens the suitcase and sifts through various pairs of underpants before selecting a white pair with some brilliant red lettering printed on the front

Jay These'll do; given me by an idiot ad man. I've never worn them.

Rose reappears through the gap

They have "Big Willie" printed on the front.
Rose (*taking them*) Oh, Jason! I do think you could have found something more suitable. (*She disappears through the curtains again*)
Jay Suitable for what? Nobody's going to dive at her knickers while she's in that condition.
Rose (*from behind the curtain*) It isn't blood. It's tomato sauce.
Jay Tomato sauce! You mean it's all a put-on?
Rose No, of course it isn't. Open the curtains.

Jay opens the curtains again. Darlene now wears the underpants. Rose is still dabbing at Darlene's face

Jay I don't get it ...
Rose There are bits of baked beans, too. The tin must have exploded.
Jay (*sitting*) Now I've heard everything. Exploding baked beans! Whoever handles Heinz's account would have a fit.
Rose (*still ministering*) There's a good girl. Oh, here's a big chunk! And it's out! (*To Jay*) She'll be fine, fine. Not even a scratch. Better, dear?
Darlene (*faintly*) Yes.
Rose Sit up and open your eyes. (*Showing Darlene a hand*) How many fingers?
Darlene Four.
Rose Well, near enough.
Jay What happened?
Darlene I was heating the beans.
Jay We guessed that, but why did the tin explode?
Darlene I forgot to put any water in the saucepan.
Rose You silly child. You might have killed yourself.
Jay (*quickly*) Let's not dwell on that.
Darlene (*getting groggily off the bed; to Rose*) Are you a doctor?
Rose No, but years ago, before you were born, I was a hospital nurse.
Darlene Thanks, anyway.
Rose Don't mention it.
Darlene I'd better be getting back. You didn't hear a phone ring?
Rose No. Enjoy your supper and don't forget the water this time!

Darlene moves to the front door

Darlene (*turning*) Have you got a saucepan?
Jay (*positively*) Yes, thanks.

Darlene hesitates, gives up, and exits, closing the front door

Rose Jason, I think she wanted to *borrow* a saucepan.
Jay I know she did.
Rose Then shouldn't you . . .?
Jay No. Lend a saucepan, lose a friend.

We hear the sound of a thumping crash and a female cry, off

Rose What's that?
Jay We may have lost a friend.

Rose leads the way through the front door. She moves R *and looks down*

Rose Are you all right!?
Darlene (*off*) I think so.
Jay What happened?
Darlene (*off*) I fell downstairs. I was going out to the shops.
Rose (*astounded*) Out?
Darlene (*off*) Yes. I'm OK.

Rose, looking dazed, comes back into the room. Jay follows, closing the front door

Rose She was going out to the shops! Dressed like that!
Jay Wasn't she wearing my "Big Willie" pants?
Rose I suppose so, but even so . . . what will people think?
Jay There you go, you see? "What will people think?" Who cares? I talk to myself. You shriek with laughter in tubes. She walks about half naked. So what? The world carries on regardless.
Rose Well, it has nothing to do with me. I suppose I should be getting along to the club.
Jay Club night, eh? And what does old George—got it!—do when you're with your deprived kids? Go out on the tiles?
Rose (*quietly*) No.
Jay Golf was his passion, wasn't it? It's all coming back. You were going to take it up, too.
Rose Two strokes.
Jay He only gives you two strokes? You must be good.
Rose He has suffered two strokes.
Jay Oh, that's too bad. How awful. Can he communicate?
Rose Yes. His brain is perfectly clear. That is half his trouble. He can't go out to work any more and resents it so terribly—just padding about the flat with nothing to do.
Jay That's where the telly is a blessing.
Rose He smashed the television set.
Jay Why?
Rose Something annoyed him.
Jay I can sympathize. The other day I threw a shoe at Esther Rantzen's teeth. Missed.
Rose (*ever cheerful*) So I'm more or less back to being a nurse again.
Jay Poor Rose.

Rose No! It's the path that God has chosen for me. Everything has a predestined purpose.

Jay You really believe that?

Rose Yes! And you will, too! You don't have to face it alone any more.

Jay Face—what?

Rose Loneliness. We are there beside you.

Jay You and old G . . . (*Pointing upwards*) Je——Him? Well, that's . . .

Rose brushes past him, goes to the desk and makes a note on a sheet of paper. Jay watches her with growing unease

Rose Every moment that I can spare, without affecting my relationship with poor George, will be devoted to you, looking after you, trying in some small way to make up for the misery I caused you. (*She goes to Jay, carrying a piece of paper, and kisses him on the cheek*) God bless you, Jason, and thank you for giving me this chance to make amends. (*She opens the front door, turns, and waves the paper*) I have your telephone number.

Rose utters one of her laughs, and exits through the front door

Jay (*with feeling*) Jesus! (*He hurries to the desk and picks up the S–Z directory*) George . . . George . . .? Shipley. (*He opens the directory and looks up the name*) Shipley, George. NW Ten. Gotcha! (*He taps out the number*) Hullo? Is that George Shipley? George! This is a voice from the past. Jay. . . . Jay Spencer. . . . (*Frowning*) Spencer! You married my . . . yes, Jason Spencer. I say, George, I was most terribly sorry to hear about your illness. . . . How did I hear? Why, from Rose, of course. When she popped in to see me this afternoon. . . . (*He reacts*) You didn't know she had? Oh! I was sure you must have discussed it. I say, I hope I haven't put my foot in it! Perhaps she came on the spur of the moment after hearing that my marriage was on the rocks. . . . You didn't know about that either? Oh! I can see I definitely have put my foot in it. Well, anyway, her visit gave my battered old morale a tremendous boost. She's a saint; but I'm worried. You know Rose and lame dogs. Well, that and this guilt complex of hers about me seems to have tempted her to take me under her wing again. . . . (*He winces slightly as if the other speaker is shouting*) Yes . . . yes . . . that is precisely. . . . I agree. . . . I think it much wiser if I don't see too much of her. Meeting her again has rekindled a whole host of emotions I believed long since dead and buried. Propinquity is a dangerous thing. It can lead from one thing to another. Well, who knows that better than you, George! . . . (*Wincing*) Yes . . . if you could lower . . . You're shouting a bit, George . . . hullo? . . . George? . . . Hullo? (*The line has gone dead. He hangs up, looking quietly satisfied with himself*) Now do we get a little peace and quiet?

The doorbell rings

No. We do not. (*He opens the front door*)

Darlene stands outside, carrying a brown paper carrier bag. She is dressed as before in the stained man's shirt. She also wears the comedy underpants. She opens her mouth and sneezes in his face

Is that all you have to say?

Darlene (*sniffing*) Excuse me. (*She sniffs*) There was a cat on the landing. Atishoo! Allergic to cats.

Darlene enters, puts down the bag, and from the breast pocket of the shirt takes out a nasal inhaler which she uses noisily

Jay Pains in her sinus,
  Stuff up her nose.
  She shall have mucus,
  Wherever she goes.
Darlene Pardon?
Jay Sorry. It's my long association with commercial jingles.
Darlene I met that nurse in the street.
Jay I bet she didn't call you a rude word.
Darlene She said: "Bless you, child, don't catch cold", and patted me on the head.
Jay Bless her!
Darlene Then—do you know what?—she rushed across the street and went and patted some strange Indian on the head. His mouth dropped right open.
Jay If you'd hung around you might have seen her shove a Malteser in his mouth. That's probably why it dropped open.
Darlene Eh?
Jay They're old friends.
Darlene Is she an old friend of yours, too?
Jay That was no friend, that was my old wife.
Darlene Another!
Jay Number one.
Darlene (*giggling*) How many have you had, then?
Jay Three so far, and no further.
Darlene Will the third one be popping in, too?
Jay (*briefly*) No. She died.
Darlene Sorry. Tck! You've had a rough time, haven't you?
Jay (*smiling*) I'm a survivor.
Darlene She seems all right this one, the nurse.
Jay More than all right. An angel.
Darlene What went wrong?
Jay Just a case of two inexperienced people marrying in haste. Wife meets older, more experienced gent, and—bingo—the earth trembles.
Darlene Did you hate the other man?
Jay At the time. Swore I'd kill him but never got around to it.
Darlene Do you still hate him?
Jay Old—thingummy? George? Good God, no! In fact I was having a lovely chat with him on the phone not two minutes ago.
Darlene (*listening*) Was that my phone? (*There is silence—she sighs*) I bought some chicken from the take-away.
Jay Wise move. Take-away chicken rarely explodes.
Darlene I wondered . . . ?

Jay If I'd lend you a knife, fork, salt, pepper, chair, what?

Darlene No. If you'd like some. I bought two portions.

Jay But for you and who?

Darlene You and me.

Jay (*surprised*) Why?

Darlene (*shrugging*) It's your first night on your own and I saw your . . . the nurse had gone so I went back and bought some more, in case.

Jay (*touched*) That was very sweet of you.

Darlene Big deal! It isn't Kentucky and the chips are gross.

Jay It's the thought—a very kind thought. (*He kisses her on the cheek*) And I'm kinky for gross chips.

Darlene *Are* you kinky?

Jay Because I kissed you on the cheek?

Darlene (*lifting her shirt to reveal the underpants*) No. Are these yours?

Jay Unwanted gift—and it's a lie anyway.

Darlene Yes, I know that.

Jay (*bridling slightly*) How would you know that?

Darlene Well, your name's not Willie, is it?

Jay Good thinking. Perceptive.

Darlene Why did you keep them, then?

Jay I'm psychic. I somehow knew I'd meet up with a knickerless girl who'd blow herself up with a tin of baked beans.

Darlene I'll warm it through, then bring it back on the trolley. (*She goes to the door, pauses, then turns*) Unless you want to be alone. I mean, you don't have to eat it with me.

Jay (*sincerely*) You *are* perceptive. I did want to be alone . . .

Darlene (*turning away*) That's all right.

Jay No. Hang on. I think a quiet fried chicken *à deux* might be just what the doctor ordered. We'll have some flat champagne to wash it down, but, darling . . .

Darlene Yes?

Jay I have an odd feeling about tonight. Not just you and me, but everyone, everything.

Darlene (*blankly*) Huh?

Jay (*pointing upwards*) It's as if that old joker up there has decided to put the new me through the wringer.

Darlene There's nobody up there. We're on the top floor.

Jay I know you women. If a man makes a pass on the first date, he's an animal. If he doesn't, he's gay. But if I don't behave according to the book in any way it's because I'm still fumbling my way through virgin territory, expecting snares, booby-traps, wolves in sheep's clothing. You know.

Darlene No. I don't know what you're talking about.

Jay Neither do I. Forget it.

Darlene I'm not a virgin, if that's what you're on about.

Jay It wasn't; but I'll file that away.

Darlene And I don't think you really are.

Jay Crazy?

Darlene No, a dirty old man.

Jay Don't count your fried chickens. Despite everything I just said, the night is yet young.

Darlene Do you fancy me, then?

Jay I haven't thought about it. (*Thinking*) I have thought about it. No. Perhaps it's that shirt. Why don't you change into something more conservative, like a star-spangled G-string?

Darlene I haven't got one.

Darlene exits with the chicken

Jay makes a little grimace, at the failure of yet another joke. He closes the front door, and moves away from it. The doorbell rings. Jay briefly closes his eyes, but betrays no emotion as usual, goes back to the front door, and opens it. He remains admirably calm

Sonia enters. She carries a white carrier bag, which is full of food cartons and also contains a bottle of rice wine

Sonia Hullo.

Jay Hullo. I thought Emanuelle was dining with Fred Fellini?

Sonia I phoned to ask him what to wear and his answering service said he'd been called away suddenly.

Jay That's a lie.

Sonia (*reacting*) What?

Jay (*covering up*) Surely, he wouldn't treat you like that?

Sonia He's always flitting off to Rome at a moment's notice. Anyway, it suited me.

Jay Did it? I don't mean to sound churlish but why should this bring you back here?

Sonia I got to thinking about that girl in the shirt.

Jay The Princess?

Sonia You didn't deny anything. You didn't say a word. You just let me assume she was your bird.

Jay So?

Sonia So, it being you, I decided you probably didn't know her after all.

Jay You read me like a book.

Sonia Then you didn't?

Jay I didn't.

Sonia Can you bear to eat Chinese? I bought some take-away.

Jay You did?

Sonia Masses, and a bottle of rice wine. Where's your kitchen?

Jay indicates the kitchen. Sonia moves in that direction

Jay Sonia——

Sonia (*cutting in*) Don't say anything yet. Let's eat, get a little sloshed, then see if we can talk without murdering each other.

Jay Yes. I hope you brought chopsticks.

Sonia No.

Sonia exits to the kitchen, closing the door

Jay Pity. Blunt instruments might have been safer. (*Going to the front door*) Farewell chicken and gross chips. (*Calling*) Darling . . . crisis . . . (*He opens the front door*)

Mary Parfitt is standing on the doorstep and Jay almost collides with her

(*Nearly losing control for the first time*) Miss Parfitt! What the hell are you doing here?

Mary is a well-educated girl with a slightly hearty, jolly-hockeysticks manner, which disguises a vulnerable personality. She is one of those girls who almost enjoy being maltreated and is easily reduced to tears. She wears a head-scarf, raincoat, thick-lensed spectacles and carries a briefcase. She looks to be a typical, rather drab secretary

Mary Oh, gosh! You're livid. I know. You wanted to be alone.

Jay So, to make absolutely sure I wasn't, you joined the gang.

Mary Gang? You mean you've had people?

Jay I certainly have had people. For a first evening in a supposedly secret hideout, I have had more people than I would have dreamed possible. So what do you want?

Mary I'd just closed the office and was on my way home when I suddenly thought . . . (*She half raises the briefcase as if she is about to refer to its contents*)

Jay I've already talked to him, if it's to do with that bloody sheik.

Mary No, it's Greek.

Jay Huh?

Mary Greek food. I was passing a take-away and thought of you on your own. (*Opening the briefcase and taking out various cartons, which she puts on the coffee table*) Humous, stuffed vine leaves, shishkebab and moussaka . . .

Jay God Almighty!

Mary I thought you might be starving.

Jay You were wrong. You don't know how wrong.

Mary's lips start to tremble. Tears are very close

Mary I'm sorry. I meant well . . .

Jay You always do. I never knew anyone who means better than you and nine times out of ten you end up being a pain in the arse.

Mary gives a sob, presses a fist to her mouth, then turns and runs into the bathroom, closing the door after her

(*As she goes*) I'm sorry. That was . . . oh, shit! Steady Spencer, we don't lose our temper any more, remember? (*He goes to the front door, opens it wide; calling across the landing*) Oi! You there!

Rose (*off*) Hellowee!

Rose enters through the front door. She carries a bulging paper bag with food containers in it. Stains of leaking curry show at the bottom. She breezes in bending forward in a playful manner

Coming up! One mild korma and one *vinda*loo-oo!

Jay slowly moves aside. One has again to admire his regained sang froid

   Did I say it right?

Jay Very nearly; except that it's vind*ah*loo.

Rose You're not cross?

Jay No. You said vin and not bin this time.

Rose I mean about my coming back? I suddenly couldn't bear the thought of you sitting here alone.

Jay Join the club, and talking of clubs, what about your deprived kiddies?

Rose They can manage without me for once.

Jay Old George, won't he . . .?

Rose He doesn't expect me back 'til ten-thirty at the earliest. So, you see, we can settle down, tuck in and have a really good natter. (*She takes the cartons to the coffee table, puts them down and just has time to register the Greek food*)

   Mary enters from the bathroom

Sonia comes out of the kitchen carrying a tray, on which are a number of cardboard cartons of Chinese food, and a bottle of rice wine

Sonia Velly, velly nice flied lice . . . (*Seeing Rose and Mary*) Oh!

   Darlene enters through the front door, pulling a food trolley on which is the chicken meal. She has abandoned the shirt, in favour of a man's pyjama top, which is open at the front. She still wears the comedy pants.

Darlene (*before turning*) I wasn't really upset, you know. It's not what you said that bugged me. I just hate my boobs being called tits.

Darlene turns and sees the others. Jay makes an apologetic gesture as——

   —the CURTAIN *falls*

ACT II

SCENE 1

The same. The action is continuous

Jay, Mary, Darlene, Rose and Sonia are in the same positions

Jay Ye-es. Now where shall we begin? Introductions! (*To Rose and Darlene*) You two ladies don't know my wonderful secretary, Miss Parfitt. If her nose is rather red it has nothing to do with you, but is because I've just been unforgiveably rude to her. Miss Parfitt, you haven't met the Princess Darlene von und zu Unterschlitzen, from the House of Hesse, who is staying incognito in Primrose Hill. (*To Rose and Sonia*) You've both met the Princess, but don't know each other. Rose — Sonia. Sonia — Rose. (*Chattily, to Mary*) Rose is my first wife.

Sonia Is this your idea of a joke?

Jay Good God, no! I could hardly have planned a situation like this, could I?

Sonia makes a sceptical grunt and puts the Chinese food cartons down on the, already laden, coffee table, which now houses Greek, Chinese and Indian food

We really do have a groaning board, don't we? Isn't this fun?

Sonia No.

Jay Sonia, are you going to spoil a unique occasion?

Sonia Yes.

Jay I was afraid you wouldn't let me down.

Darlene I'll go.

Sonia Good.

Darlene makes a move as if to go

Jay (*stopping her*) Woa! Come back! You're staying. (*Sotto voce*) Please. I want you to.

Rose I think I should be getting along.

Sonia Good!

Jay Sonia!

Sonia I want to talk to you *alone*.

Jay That makes a change but you do seem to have chosen the worst evening in five years.

Sonia Not if certain people show a little tact.

Rose (*to Jay*) If "certain people" refers to me, I shall be happy to leave you.

Sonia As you were when you ditched him eighteen years ago.

Rose (*with dignity*) I shall ignore that.

Sonia I'll bet you will! I'd just like to know who, or what, has called you out of the mothballs after two decades?

Mary (*suddenly*) I think we should *all* go.

Sonia You mind your own bloody business, Miss Parfitt.

Mary I don't have to take that kind of talk from you any longer, Mrs Spencer.

Sonia Oh, get lost! Look, your sheep's eyes at Jay have been a standing joke for the last five years. It's got you nowhere so far and it won't change now; so just buzz off, will you?

Jay Sonia, you're excelling yourself.

Sonia Wait!

Mary I shall not leave until my employer requests me to.

Sonia Don't bet on that, sweetie.

Darlene (*hopping from one foot to the other and raising a hand, schoolgirl fashion*) I want to go.

Jay (*pointing*) Bathroom's through there, darling.

Darlene No. Away. Out.

Jay Absolutely not. The way things are shaping we may need a neutral referee.

Sonia Neutral! Ha!

Jay Sonia, I'm naturally flattered by this display of jealous outrage ...

Sonia Jealous! Of anything here?

Jay Do be logical. If I'd planned something with the Princess I'd hardly have invited Rose or Miss Parfitt. Conversely, had Rose and I planned a nostalgic get-together I wouldn't have invited Miss Parfitt or ...

Sonia You didn't invite me either. It's obvious. The old-timer, the typist and I screwed up your sordid little plans with (*jerking a finger at Darlene*) that.

Jay Actually, I'd planned an early night *alone*, so all four of you can be said to have screwed that up.

Sonia (*to Darlene*) And where do you live, dear?

Darlene Here.

Jay When she says "here", she doesn't mean here. (*Pointing*) Across the landing.

Sonia How handy!

Jay Isn't it? I shall for ever be popping across to sample her supersoft marge, admire her sparkling dishes, her whiter than whites and, of course, to compare my Kit-e-Kat with her Whiskas.

Darlene And I'm not a Princess.

Sonia No—too obviously a commoner.

Darlene You're very rude, aren't you?

Sonia You have struck me on one of my ruder days.

Darlene I heard that in the street. You should wash your mouth out.

Sonia You believe in washing. Now that surprises me.

Darlene (*moving in*) And you've got me on a day when I don't mind what I do. (*Cocking two fingers*) So I might just stick my fingers up your snotty nose.

Sonia As a change from being up your own, perhaps?

Rose (*disgusted*) Really! I might as well be at my club.

Jay They talk like that at your club! Oh! The deprived tots! Yes, they would.

Rose Either, as Miss Parfitt says, we should all leave, or we should endeavour to keep the conversation on a civilized level.

Jay Well said! Look, all four of you, independently, played the Good Samaritan. I'm really touched. It would be a pity if these Christian acts developed into a slanging match.

Sonia Why?

Jay Once epithets are flung, hard objects surely follow. As a practised plate thrower you should know that.

Sonia I enjoy throwing plates.

Jay Then throw old Carlo's. I'm very short.

Darlene The food'll be getting cold.

Jay She's right. Before we get too heated let's cool off and eat the food while it's warm. All in favour say ay!

Nobody says anything

Unanimous! Right! We shall now eat. (*To Mary*) Do take off your raincoat, Miss Parfitt.

Mary removes her raincoat and head-scarf but still wears her thick glasses. Rose unstacks the Indian food containers, and starts arranging them on the coffee table. Sonia starts to arrange the Chinese cartons on the coffee table. Mary joins them and tries to get a fair deal for her Greek food. Lastly Darlene joins the fray with two plates on which are chicken and chips. A vicious struggle now ensues, rising to a crescendo, as each woman tries to get fair space for her meal. One of the results is that a plate of chicken and chips gets knocked to the floor and Darlene has to pick the pieces up and replace them on the plate. The whole battle is accompanied by a series of "Excuse me's", "Do you mind's?", "Look out's!", "Well, really's!" etc. It develops into a situation where fisticuffs become a virtual certainty. Jay is seen to move away and search for something in the tea-chest. Now he returns and suddenly, to great effect, blows a loud blast on a whistle. The struggle stops. Everyone looks at him

(*Showing them the whistle*) Snatched this off a West Ham supporter who kept blowing it every time Arsenal looked like scoring last Saturday. That's better, ladies. We don't want to eat off the floor, do we?

Rose Should I get some cutlery?

Jay Thanks. It's in a drawer by the sink.

Rose exits into the kitchen, closing the door after her

Mary kneels down by the coffee table and starts to pick up a few chips from the floor

Darlene (*moving away*) Excuse me. I forgot the tomato sauce.

Jay You're to come back. Promise!

Darlene nods and exits through the front door

Sonia places her cartons to advantage. She picks up a carton of Greek food and looks into it

Sonia (*shuddering*) Ugh! Is this to eat or has it already been eaten?

Mary (*coldly*) That is moussaka. (*She tries to snatch the carton away*)

Sonia, almost certainly with intent, contrives that the carton spills into Mary's face and down the front of her dress before (hopefully) falling on to the table and not the floor. Mary jumps up with a cry

Sonia Oh, butterfingers!

Mary You did that on purpose! I can't stand it! I'm sorry! I can't take this any more. (*Rescuing her raincoat and scarf, she stumbles towards the door, stifling sobs*) I'll see you at the office tomorrow—sir.

Jay (*halfway to the door*) Yes . . . I . . . sorry . . . thanks for the Greek thought . . . most kind . . .

Mary exits through the front door

Jay turns to Sonia, who looks quietly satisfied

How could you?

Sonia (*grimly*) Easy. One down and two to go.

Jay Sonia, you're to stop this.

Sonia I'm warning you, laddie. If you don't get the old cow and that young tart out of here, *I* will, and I don't care how I do it.

Jay You are unbelievable.

Sonia *I* am? It must be the change of life.

Jay Come on! You'd have a hot flush if someone stuffed moussaka in your face.

Sonia Not Parfitt. I mean that scrubber. You creaking around with that! You're old enough to be her grandfather.

Jay (*peeking into one of the Chinese food cartons*) Balls! (*Looking up*) Meatballs! My favourite!

Sonia Did you hear what I said?

Jay The grandfather bit! You're over preoccupied with age. Rose is old. This one's young. I'm having the change. Nothing any of us can do about it, so why bring it up?

Sonia Have you really looked at it, listened to it? Ugh!

Jay You don't approve? Pity. If Darlene and I decide to marry I'd planned on you and Rose being matrons of honour.

Sonia picks up a carton of Chinese food and is about to smash it over his head. Jay wrestles with her

Rose enters from the kitchen, carrying four forks

Jay and Sonia desist

Rose I could only find four forks . . .

Jay Spoons are in a Cadbury's Milk Tray box on top of the oven. I didn't unpack them yet.

Rose exits into the kitchen again

(*Looking into the carton which Sonia has just put down*) Fish balls, too! You're spoiling me. Glad you didn't clout me with those.

Sonia At least tell me what that old cow is doing here?

Jay She's not that old. She's younger than me—and look how you're starting to fancy me all over again.

Sonia What's she *doing* here?

Jay She just turned up.

Sonia Because you sent for her.

Jay No.

Sonia (*triumphantly*) Liar! How would she know where to find you?

Jay Like you, she used a detective. It's true. Ask her. Fellow by the name of Murphy, absolute wizard.

Sonia God, I loathe you in this repellent good humour.

Jay Too bad, because it's a fixture. (*With a deliberately irritating smile*) And don't worry about Rose. You're a much bigger threat to our marriage than she'll ever be.

Sonia seizes the rice wine bottle and wields it like a club

Rose enters, carrying some spoons with the forks

Rose Found the spoons but I couldn't see any knives.

Jay Then some of us may yet survive the evening.

Rose (*putting the cutlery on the coffee table; with intent*) The dear old kitchen—just the same.

Sonia What does that mean?

Jay (*hastily*) It's a very dear old kitchen, badly in need of decoration.

Rose Oh come along, Jason! (*To Sonia*) Didn't he tell you? This was our home after we married.

Sonia (*nearly dropping the bottle*) Was it indeed? Well! Well! And whose brilliant notion was it to return?

Jay According to Rose——(*jerking a thumb skywards*) His.

Sonia Whose?

Jay Him.

Sonia Some man upstairs?

Jay *The* man upstairs. The Big Cheese. Divine Providence. And He's having a divine time mixing it tonight, isn't He?

Rose (*to Jay*) I stupidly forgot to buy chapatis or pappodoms, and I couldn't find any bread in there.

Jay The bread's in the waste-bin.

Rose The waste-bin!

Jay I don't have a bread bin; but not to worry, I haven't produced any waste either.

Jay exits into the kitchen

Rose (*opening the Indian food cartons; singing*) "All things bright and beautiful, all creatures great and small . . ."

Sonia If I could interrupt the audition, Miss Melba.

Rose (*speaking*) You said something? (*Singing*) "All things bright and beautiful. The Lord God made them all."

Sonia Regardless of anything you've heard, Jay and I are still married and I intend to keep it that way.

Rose (*singing*) "All things wise and wonderful . . ."

Sonia So you're making a big mistake if you're planning a comeback.

Rose (*speaking*) Plates! I forgot plates!

Sonia You don't stand an earthly. You've seen his scrubber. Even I'm long in the tooth for him.

Rose It's a little cooler today, don't you think?

Sonia Bollocks.

Rose (*smiling*) Interesting. In my classes it is always the disturbed children who use four letter words.

Sonia That was a seven letter word.

Rose Eight, actually. The word bollock on its own has seven letters. You said bollocks. That is eight.

Sonia If you prefer nine—arseholes.

Rose (*confidentially*) I never let it shock me. It is only a rather pathetic plea for attention.

Sonia Then may I grab your attention, teacher?

Rose Certainly.

Sonia I don't believe in Divine Providence, so I'd like a straight answer to the question—what are you cooking up?

Rose I don't understand.

Sonia Come on! Jay didn't return here by accident, did he?

Rose Ask him. I played no part in it.

Sonia So how come you're here? Did he call you?

Rose If you must know I hired a man called Murphy to . . .

Sonia (*staggered*) My God! It's true! You did . . .

Jay enters from the kitchen with a tray, on which are four glasses, some plates, a large flat oval dish, the loaf of rye bread and a pepper pot—the model which one shakes to obtain pepper

Darlene enters at the same time as Jay. She is carrying a tomato ketchup bottle with about an eighth of an inch of ketchup in it

Rose (*to Jay*) Ah, you remembered the plates, Jason.

Jay Let's picnic round the coffee table. Don't want to be too formal, do we?

Darlene There isn't much tomato sauce.

Jay Suits me. You showed me enough today to last me a lifetime. Rose, why don't you sit on the sofa. (*To Darlene*) You take the pouffe.

Rose and Darlene sit as instructed. Rose on the R end of the sofa. Jay picks up the bottle of rice wine and hands it to Sonia

Sonia, you do the honours. Nothing like a drop of rice wine to break the ice.

Sonia (*undoing the top of the wine*) Or a skull.

Jay takes two glasses and hands one to Rose and the other to Darlene

Darlene (*sneezing*) Did you say rice wine?

Jay Yes, you must try it—great decongestant. Blows your head off.

Sonia walks behind the sofa, stops right behind and above Rose and raises the bottle with the obvious intention of emptying it on Rose's head. Jay, moving like lightning, lunges forward and seizes the bottle from her in the nick of time

Rose (*quite unaware of this and looking in the other direction*) Where is Miss Parfitt?
Jay Um—she had a bit of a turn. She's gone home.

Sonia, foiled for the moment, sits on the other end of the sofa with a glass in her hand. Jay pours her some

Rose Oh, dear. Of course. She has this heart problem, you said.
Sonia Bleeding—plus a surfeit of sheep's eyes.
Rose She ate sheep's eyes?
Sonia No. She makes them.

Jay starts to pour Rose some wine

Rose (*covering her glass*) No!
Jay Of course. Sorry. (*He goes to pour Darlene some wine*)
Sonia It isn't poison, you know.
Rose It is to me. I never drink.

Jay moves L, gets rid of the wine and stands L of the coffee table

Jay Now, then, (*rattling it off*) we have fried chicken, soggy chips, crispy noodles, yellow rice, white rice, mixed dry vegetables, mild korma, hot vindaloo, humous, shishkebab, stuffed vine leaves, spare ribs, meat balls, fish balls, sweet and sour pork, one portion mango chutney, bean shoots, three lychees . . . three? We'll have to draw lots and finally a smattering, not to say spattering, of moussaka. Come and get it!

Darlene is the first to the table and picks up one of the plates of chicken and chips. She turns away

No curry?
Darlene Ooh, no! My grandad was in the Indian army and he said no-one in India eats curry at night.
Jay You mean that seven hundred million poor Indians are always sent to bed without their supper?
Darlene (*returning to the pouffe*) Oh, I don't know about the *Indians*. For all I know they don't eat curry, anyway.
Jay Why do you think they cook it, then?
Darlene Because it's cheap and makes a change from Big Macs.
Jay One lives and learns. Sonia, a little of both curries?
Sonia I loathe and detest curry.
Jay One verb would have been enough. Help yourself to Greek or Chinese, then.

Sonia helps herself to some Chinese food, making a fairly full plate. She returns to the sofa

Rose, a bit of everything?
Rose (*approaching the table hesitantly*) No. I—I don't fancy anything just for the moment. I feel a little dicky.

Sonia snorts delightedly, chokes and spits out some food

Sonia No comment.

Rose (*coldly*) I have a hiatus hernia.

Jay I've never known exactly what a hiatus hernia is.

Rose (*enthusiastically*) Inflammation of the muscle fibres round the oesophagus. They become slack, causing the contents of the stomach, with acid, to regurgitate upwards, resulting in pain, wind . . .

Sonia (*banging her spoon on her plate*) Do you mind?

Jay Yes, perhaps we should gurgitate before we regurgitate.

Rose moves back and stands in front of her place at the sofa. Jay is helping himself to food, and thus does not see Sonia deliberately place her plate of food on the sofa so that Rose will inevitably sit on it

Darlene I don't like spicy food. Curries make me sweat.

Rose starts to sit, stops, and straightens up to take up Darlene's line

Rose Now, isn't that strange! My husband is the same! Two mouthfuls of curry and his shirt is sopping. (*To Jay*) I told you.

Darlene And I think I'm allergic to Chinese.

Rose starts to sit again, but, once more, straightens up in the nick of time—to Sonia's chagrin

Rose Don't talk to me about allergies! I only have to sniff at a prawn to come out in a horrid rash.

Rose now sits, but to Sonia's fury, she sits on the arm of the couch and not on the food

(*Confidentially*) Under the arms.

Darlene Chinese prawns give me spots, huge lumpy ones.

Rose My rash just itches.

Sonia And cabbage makes me fart.

Jay Sonia!

Sonia (*moving away; disgusted*) Well, do we have to listen to these sick-making revelations while we're eating?

Jay Nothing's going to put me off.

Sonia reverts to chewing her nails. During the ensuing scene, Jay helps himself to ample portions of the food of three nations, then sits in the armchair. Darlene picks up the pepper pot and prepares to shake pepper over her chicken

Careful of that pepper pot.

Darlene, shaking the pepper pot, looks towards Jay, and fails to notice that the top falls off, resulting in an avalanche of pepper pouring out into the carton

Darlene Why?

Jay The top comes off.

Darlene Oh. (*Looking down and seeing that it has*) Oh! (*She rescues the top and gazes glumly into the carton. She goes to the dining-table and tries to remove the excess pepper with a paper napkin*)

Sonia bites her nails

Jay (*to Sonia*) With so much food on offer must you chew your nails?
Sonia They're my nails.
Jay I'm not suggesting anyone else would care to sample them. What's left of them.

As an alternative to the nails, Sonia produces her cigarettes, sticks one in her mouth and lights it

Rose (*watching Sonia hungrily*) I—ah—wonder if I might borrow a cigarette?
Sonia Borrow? Sure, but return it tomorrow by nine a.m. or I'll send in the bailiffs. Borrow!

She chucks the packet and lighter on to Rose's lap

Jay (*surprised*) Rose! You smoking?
Rose I—ah—have the odd one ... occasionally ... when ... it settles the nerves ... when one doesn't drink ... (*She lights the cigarette. She is an amateur smoker, who holds the cigarette between the forefinger and thumb and tends to crook the little finger. She draws a small amount of smoke and puffs it out without inhaling, in short, nervous, audible blasts*)
Sonia (*moving past Rose to stand* C, *below the sofa*) I insist on saying something.

There is a silence

And I won't be interrupted.
Jay You have the floor, comrade.

Rose now inhales deeply and audibly

Sonia The fact that Jay and I may have problems, is nobody's business but our own. (*To Rose*) Right?

Rose opens her mouth to say something, which causes inhaled smoke to go the wrong way. She is seized with a loud and continuous paroxysm of coughing. Visibly irritated, Sonia waits for the paroxysm to pass

Rose (*gasping*) Wrong way ... that's better. Oh!
Sonia Accepting this, is it unreasonable ...?

Darlene is looking closely into the pepper-laden carton, trying to pick out pieces which may be edible. Suddenly she lets out a tremendous sneeze, which silences Sonia, who waits, then begins to talk again

Accepting this, is it ...?

Rose gets a renewed fit of coughing and Darlene starts sneezing uncontrollably. Jay desperately tries to maintain a serious and attentive face

Darlene Atishoo! Pepper! Atishoo!
Rose (*gasping*) Would someone please take this ... (*She waves the guilty cigarette in the air*)

Jay takes it away from her and stubs it out. Darlene presses a finger to the end of her nose, in the fashion recommended to prevent sneezing. Rose appears to recover. Sonia, wary of getting caught again, looks from one to the other. Jay's mouth begins to twitch as he looks at all three women

Sonia Accepting this . . .

Jay loses his battle against laughter. It bursts out of him through his clenched teeth with a noise like tearing paper. His efforts to restrain it result in a fit of coughing. Sonia says something mercifully inaudible and glares at him

Jay Terribly sorry . . . regurgitated . . . (*He controls himself*)

Darlene presses her nose. Rose's mouth is clamped shut

Sonia Has everyone had their fun? Quite finished?

Darlene nods. Jay nods. Sonia looks at Rose whose volcano is obviously still active, since she occasionally gives a convulsive heave. She opens her mouth, lets out one strangled word, then clamps it shut again

Rose Water.
Darlene I'll fetch some.

 Darlene exits into the kitchen

Sonia and Jay both look at Rose. Rose's cheeks slowly inflate as she battles to stop another outbreak. Her eyes bulge. Her face suffuses with blood. Then the crisis seems to pass. Gradually Rose deflates and her face reverts to normal. Jay and Sonia relax visibly. Rose draws a deep breath, smiles triumphantly, starts to speak then goes straight into the loudest paroxysm of all. Sonia beats her own forehead with her fists and stamps her feet like a child

Rose (*staggering to her feet*) Choking . . . can't breathe.

Jay seizes a glass of rice wine and thrusts it into Rose's hand

Jay Drink that.

 Darlene enters from the kitchen with a jug of water

Rose tilts the glass back, and practically drains it at a gulp. The effect is catastrophic. Her face distorts. She utters a strangled cry

Rose (*hoarsely*) What was that?
Jay (*unthinkingly*) Rice wine.
Rose Aaaah!

The action which follows takes place very fast and some of it is simultaneous. As this action takes place the following dialogue is spoken but not necessarily entirely heard

Rose You gave me wine! Must go . . . Home . . . George . . .
Jay God, I'm sorry, Rose. Didn't think . . .
Sonia Kill you . . . Wait, just you wait . . .

Rose flings out both arms in a desperate gesture of dismay. This results in her inadvertantly pushing Sonia violently backwards, so that she collapses into the sofa and sits plumb on the plate of food she has set as a trap for Rose, with disastrous results to the back of her skirt. Sonia leaps to her feet with a yell of pure rage, seizes the plate and wields it lethally

Darlene simply panics and scuttles out through the front door, to the safety of her own flat, carrying the water jug. Rose grabs her handbag and runs to the front door where she exits, babbling incoherently

Jay combines evading being brained by Sonia, with a half-hearted pursuit of Rose to the front door, uttering apologies. This is followed by a further brush with Sonia who pushes Darlene's trolley at him

Sonia exits through the front door

After Sonia has gone Jay closes the front door and lets out a long sigh

Jay Is it possible? Are we alone at last?

The doorbell rings

It is not possible. Mad fool. (*Calling*) Who goes there?

We hear a sneeze; off

Oh! What do you want?
Darlene (*off; muffled*) Waa ta gay ma towy.
Jay What?
Darlene (*off; muffled*) Waa ta gay ma towy.

Jay shakes his head, then opens the front door

Darlene enters, still carrying the water jug

Jay What do you want?
Darlene My trolley, and here's your jug.

Jay takes the jug

(*Going to the trolley*) Sorry I ran away, but I thought she was going to murder you.
Jay I was sure she was. Don't know why she didn't try harder. Violence stimulates her. Some of our rare successes in the sack have followed assaults with a deadly weapon.
Darlene What was it—jealousy?
Jay Oh, no! I provided all the jealousy.
Darlene Was she unfaithful, then?
Jay Let's say Sonia took a rather wide view of the straight and narrow.
Darlene (*giggling*) Did you do it on purpose?
Jay What?
Darlene Give one the wine and make the other sit on her dinner.
Jay Not guilty, I swear; but it did bring a nice swift end to the proceedings. Sorry to have involved you but I didn't want to be left alone with any of them—not tonight.
Darlene She's potty about you, isn't she?
Jay Sonia? No ...

Darlene No. The other. Your secretary.

Jay Parfitt? No! I think a lot of secretaries develop a dog-like devotion, but it's nothing more than that.

Darlene You probably never look at the poor thing, but I did, and I think she's potty about you.

Jay Nice to think someone is.

Darlene (*pushing the trolley towards the front door*) Goodbye.

Jay Let's make that good-night. I don't like goodbyes from you. They lead to explosions.

Darlene exits

(*He closes the front door, then goes to pour himself a drink, humming the old song "Alone"*) "Alone, alone tum-tee-tum-tee-tee-tee. Alone! There must be someone . . ."

The doorbell rings

Ringing the way they always do. (*He puts down his drink, goes to the front door and opens it*)

Darlene stands outside

That was a short night.

Darlene I thought if I gave it a good scrub it would warm up nicely.

There is quite a long pause while Jay digests this statement

Jay I wish I knew what we were talking about.

Darlene My chicken with the pepper all over it.

Jay Ah!

Darlene So could I have my tomato sauce?

He nods, but they do not move. Their eyes meet and hold. They are still looking at each other as the Lights fade to Black-out

CURTAIN

SCENE 2

The same. Later that night

When the CURTAIN rises the stage is empty. It is now night, and the only illumination comes from night light through the windows and from the electric light in the kitchen. The bed has a duvet and sheet untidily heaped on it

Jay enters from the kitchen. He wears a short dressing-gown and carries a mug, from which he sips. He again hums the song "Alone". He turns on the room lights. He looks at himself approvingly in the mirror

Jay "Alone . . . tum-tum-tum . . ."

Darlene (*from under the duvet*) You're a fraud, you are.

Jay Huh?

The duvet moves and Darlene's head appears

Darlene "I don't need anybody", he says!

Jay (*joining Darlene on the bed*) I didn't need you, my darling. I wanted you. Two quite different things. I didn't need this coffee, but I wanted it.

Darlene So I'm just a coffee.

Jay Sweeter. I've run out of sugar.

Darlene I wonder what they'd say?

Jay Who?

Darlene Your wives, Don Juan!

Jay Sonia would try to kill me, of course. Rose would understand. That's her. Always thinking of others, never of herself. The truth is, she probably finds the others more amusing.

Darlene And the one who died? What . . .?

Jay (*briefly*) Car crash.

Darlene Tck! Poor thing and poor you.

Jay None of that, now. I'm not sorry for myself and I don't want anybody else feeling sorry for me.

Darlene (*heaving one of her more telling sighs*) Some of us are just born to be unlucky.

Jay None of that either. If you hope, because you're nosy about my past, that I'm going to listen to your boring troubles, you're mistaken.

Darlene You really are weird.

Jay Did you think about your problems while we were making love?

Darlene Of course not!

Jay Why not?

Darlene You looking for compliments?

Jay No—so why not?

Darlene Well—you took my mind off it.

Jay No, *you* did. The last thing I thought about was your mind.

Darlene So I forgot, but you can't help things coming back.

Jay (*getting launched*) Don't you see, you can! And it's taken me three quarters of my life to discover that. You can do anything you want. It's your head. Everything that goes into it *you* put there. Anything you don't like you can chuck out.

Darlene You sound like a preacher.

Jay (*kissing her lightly*) Your very own lay preacher.

Darlene (*laying her head on Jay's shoulder*) I say, Jay. Was I——?

Jay (*cutting in*) Aha! That is approval seeking—a mortal sin in the gospel according to St Jay. You can waste half your life worrying about what people think of you.

Darlene Everyone worries about that.

Jay Not me. I'm now prepared to be cordially detested so long as *I* approve of what I do. (*Kissing her again*) Just this once, though, let me say you were lovely.

Darlene You were great. I could fancy you rotten.

Jay Not too rotten, darling.

Darlene Why?

Jay I told you. I'm playing it cautious, avoiding ties, complications.

Darlene Doesn't sound natural to me. If I like making it with someone I want to be with them all the time.

Jay And there lies disaster. Take you and me. What could have been nicer? But if you showed the slightest signs of getting hooked ...

Darlene (*totally sincerely*) Oh, you don't have to worry about that. I'd never fall in love with you. You're much too old.

He digests this and finally nods his head

Jay I think I like that. I'm not sure, but I think I do.

The doorbell rings

(*Jumping to his feet*) Now who the hell is that? Can't be one of the merry wives back. Can it? (*He closes the curtains using the control box*) I know you have every right to be here but I couldn't stand another wounded look tonight. Try not to sneeze.

There is a second ring on the doorbell

(*Approaching the front door*) Who's there?

A woman's muffled and unrecognizable voice says something. Jay shakes his head, then opens the door

Mary stands outside. She wears her spectacles, head-scarf and raincoat. Her raincoat is soaked and spattered with mud. One of the lenses of her spectacles also has mud on it. She looks thoroughly miserable

Oh, no!

Mary Are you alone?

Jay Why?

Mary Thank God!

Mary pushes past him into the room before he can make any move to prevent her

Jay What the hell happened to you?

Mary I fell into a great hole in the road. They should have left a warning lamp ...

Jay (*impatiently*) Tough luck, but couldn't this news have waited until tomorrow?

Mary No.

She removes her raincoat and scarf, and finally puts her spectacles aside, shaking her hair out. She may hope that in doing this, she instantly becomes an irresistible sex symbol, but sadly this is not the case. She remains a very ordinary-looking girl, with the added disadvantage that she now cannot see a thing without her spectacles. She suddenly seizes Jay and pulls him into a fierce embrace

Jay (*giving an alarmed look towards the bed, and struggling to free himself*) No ... not now ...

Mary Yes, now. Cyril found out.

Jay (*blankly*) Cyril?

Mary My husband.

Jay Husband? You're married?

Mary You know I'm married! You sent us a wonderful wedding present.

Jay Did I? Yes. Of course. But found out? (*Glancing towards the bed again*) About today? The office? (*Lowering his voice*) Lunchtime today?

Mary Yes, and he's threatening to kill us.

Jay Well, thank *you*, Miss Parfitt! Very thoughtful to come here if he's charging after you.

Mary Oh, no! He doesn't know about this place. He's more likely to be bashing down the front door of your house right now. Strong as an ox.

Jay (*bewildered*) B-but how? It's impossible. You've worked for me for five years . . .

Mary *Six* years and three days . . .

Jay All right! And to be brutally frank, I've never looked at you, let alone laid a finger on you, until today.

Mary I've wanted you to, so much.

Jay That's besides the point. The fact is, there's never been a hint of anything until we sunk that damned bottle of champagne . . .

Mary I'm so glad we did . . .

Jay Please! So what happened? Did you confess, or what?

Mary No. You won't believe it when I tell you.

Jay (*giving another glance at the bed*) Wait, let's continue this conversation in the kitchen.

Mary Why?

Jay Why? Um—it doesn't smell of curry.

Mary I love the smell of curry. It's so sexy.

Jay Oh. (*Giving up*) OK, so how did he find out?

Mary Think of the most way-out, far-fetched reason, then double it.

Jay I'm in no mood for guessing games.

Mary Tonight, Cyril and I were undressing to go to bed. I took off my bra and . . . (*her voice trails away*) and . . .

Jay Go on.

Mary Your American Express Card fell out of it.

Jay Out of your *bra*?

Mary The right cup.

Jay (*flatly*) My American Express Card was in the right cup of your bra.

Mary It fell out and dropped at his feet. At first Cyril thought it was mine and said: "That's not where to put American Express. That's for Access." That was a joke.

Jay You obviously married him for his wit.

Mary Then he picked it up and saw it was yours.

Jay It's crazy. Even if you'd done it for money I wouldn't have paid by credit card.

Mary I think I know what happened. You remember we undressed in a hurry? God, that was exciting! Well, I chucked my bra on your desk. Your card must have been lying there and, later, when I picked up the bra to put it on again, I swept the card up with it.

Jay And I thought my luck had turned.

Mary I'm worried.

Jay You're worried? *I'm* worried but I'm not *supposed* to be worried. I was never going to be worried again by anything or anyone, ever.

Mary I meant I'm worried about my state of mind. Let's face it. I'm in the most ghastly mess. My marriage is on the rocks. Cyril is capable of murder and yet, coming back here, all I could think about was you, being with you.

Jay Yes, that's all very ...

Mary If things had turned out differently I'd have tried to hide it but there's no point now. We may as well face it.

Jay What?

Mary I love you. I think I always have, but now, after today, I know. I only married Cyril because I thought there was no hope of us ever ...

Jay Not so fast. You're turning a simple one——

Mary (*cutting in*) Do you believe in predestination?

Jay No, I don't! Don't you start that, too.

Mary You leave Sonia. We make love. Cyril finds out. All in a matter of hours. Can't you see what that means?

Jay Yes. One or both of us will die—violently.

Mary winces with pain, exercises her dirtied hands, raises her skirts slightly to reveal that her fall has caused holes in her stockings at the knees and that her knees are larded with mud

Mary I'm absolutely filthy. Do you mind if I have a quick bath?

Jay Yes, I do! I want you out of here.

Mary (*her eyes filling with tears*) You can't begrudge me a bath. Look at me.

Jay (*hastily*) All right! Take a bath but spare me the waterworks, please.

Mary (*recovering fast*) Thanks. (*She hurries away and trips over the pouffe, which she obviously cannot see*)

Muttering something unrepeatable Jay helps her up

Sorry! Idiot! I'm as blind as a bat without my glasses.

Jay Why don't you wear them, then?

Mary You said I looked gorgeous without them.

Jay (*impatiently*) That was in bed.

Mary No! On the office rug! God, that was fantastic!

Mary exits into the bathroom, briefly colliding with the framework of the door

The door closes behind her. We hear the bath water running. Darlene's head appears between the curtains in front of the bed. She is wrapped in a sheet

Darlene (*imitating Jay*) "Just a dog-like devotion." You liar!

Jay (*moving swiftly to Darlene, seizing her by the arm and heading her towards the front door*) I'd rather be with you, but nothing short of a bomb is going to shift her. So good-night.

Darlene On the office rug, too! Randy old man, aren't you?

Jay At this moment—no; but if I'm forced to be unfaithful to you so early in our relationship, I'm sorry.

Darlene After all you've been up to today will you be *able* to, more like!
Jay What a practical little thing you are. You shall be the first to know.
Darlene (*giggling*) No—the second.

As Jay is about to open the front door, the doorbell rings. He wheels Darlene round and heads her back towards the bed

  Who'll that be?
Jay The neighbours, to complain I'm running a brothel.

Jay pushes Darlene back between the curtains and out of sight. He hurries to the bathroom door and knocks. It opens

  Mary puts her head out. Bath water is heard running louder

(*Whispering*) Turn off the water. Someone's rung the doorbell.
Mary Cyril! No, he wouldn't ring. He kicks doors in.

  Mary disappears into the bathroom and closes the door behind her. The bathwater ceases to run

Jay (*going to the front door*) I can't wait to meet Cyril.

The doorbell rings again

Darlene (*sticking her head out, between the curtains*) You are psychic.
  Remember what you said about that joker up there putting you through
  the wringer . . .
Jay Belt up and keep quiet. (*He angrily waves her away*)

Darlene withdraws her head. During the following, still wrapped in the sheet, she opens the alcove window wide and then hides behind the bed. Jay opens the front door

  Sonia, who has changed her clothes, stands outside. She wields a large pair of scissors, and leaps at Jay with a furious cry

They enter the room, struggling. The scissors drop to the floor and Jay gives a yell of pain

(*Looking at his hand: shocked*) Look! I'm bleeding! You stabbed me!
Sonia (*yelling*) That's what I was trying to do, you bloody fool!
Jay (*obviously hating the sight of blood, particularly his own, he goes towards the bathroom*) Stay there. Don't come in.
Sonia I hope you lie there and bleed to death.

  Jay enters the bathroom, closing the door

Sonia's anger dissolves into tears. She briefly parts the curtains and hurls herself, sobbing, on to the bed. The curtains close behind her. Surprisingly, there is no outburst of rage as she, presumably, discovers Darlene

  Jay comes out of the bathroom, smoothing down a Band-Aid

A wracking cry from behind the curtains causes him to freeze. Assuming that the worst has happened, he nervously parts the curtains and looks through. He closes the curtains. He looks dumbfounded, as he switches on the control box, and the curtains part to reveal Sonia lying on the bed, her head buried. There is no sign of Darlene. Still extremely puzzled, Jay mounts the rostrum. He gives an audible gasp as he sees that the window in the alcove is wide open. He rushes into the alcove, goes the window, and looks out and down towards the ground

(*Sitting up on one elbow, looking at Jay; puzzled*) What are you doing?

Jay You didn't see or hear—um—anything fall out of this window?

Sonia Huh? What?

Jay Nothing. So, to what do I owe the attempted assassination?

Sonia (*rising and moving to Jay*) You called Carlo.

Jay You told me he was out of town.

Sonia I drove past his flat and saw a light. He was there. You stabbed me in the back.

Jay You're a fine one to talk about stabbing—and I didn't. All right, I did call him—but only to wish you both the best of luck.

Sonia You cunning bastard.

Jay You told me Carlo was madly in love with you. Of course, if that was one of your lies he might well panic and turn nasty.

Sonia Oh, he did! Coldly and clinically you sabotaged me starring in that film.

Jay Sonia, grow up! You were never in with a chance. You fell for the oldest line in the business; a classic case of the casting couch. Whether it was today, or in three months' time, you'd have been out on your ear, well and truly screwed in every sense of the word.

Sonia You're enjoying this, aren't you?

Jay (*wearily; sincerely*) What do I gain from seeing you make a fool of yourself?

Sonia Revenge.

Jay For what?

Sonia (*cutting in*) Look, I know I've been impossible to live with but that had nothing to do with competing or my career. I think it was because I'd gradually grown to despise you.

Jay Really? Fascinating.

Sonia You have this clever knack of winning everyone's sympathy, presenting yourself as one of life's victims, who never complains, always comes up smiling; but, one day, someone is going to puncture you.

Jay (*picking up the fallen scissors and proffering them to Sonia*) No-one can say you didn't try.

Sonia (*ignoring the scissors*) The first time I went to bed with you did you think of me as an easy lay?

Jay I didn't give it that much thought.

Sonia (*with sudden emphasis*) Maybe you should have since you were cosily married to Janet at the time.

Jay (*after a pause*) It takes two to make a love affair.

Sonia But everyone knows I'm a slag! It's life's gallant old victim we're talking about.

Jay You are talking about. Where is this leading?

Sonia Towards a slip of your halo, perhaps.

Jay I never professed to wear halo and, frankly, I'm getting a little bored with this inquest.

Sonia Talking of inquests, Janet found out about us, didn't she?

Jay starts to speak, but Sonia cuts in

Don't deny it. She telephoned to tell me exactly what she thought of me, ten minutes before taking her car out and ramming it into that wall.

There is a long pause

Jay You've taken a long time to come up with this sensational theory.

Sonia Yes. I waited. I was sure you'd come out with it one day, between us, but you didn't, and the rot started when I realized you felt no sense of guilt and, what's worse, basked in the sympathy everyone doled out.

Jay I wonder why you ever married me.

Sonia So, my love, do I. (*She twitches the scissors out of his hand*)

Jay half makes as if to stop her

(*Moving the scissors out of his reach*) Don't worry. I'm not going to kill myself. You're not worth it. (*She goes to the front door*)

Jay (*almost shouting*) She didn't kill herself!

Sonia (*turning at the door, smiling, plainly pleased with the effect she has had on him*) I didn't say she did. I said *I* wasn't going to. Sleep well — but then I'm sure you always do.

Sonia exits, shutting the front door behind her

Darlene's head pops up from behind the bed. She is still wrapped in the sheet

Darlene I say . . .

Jay (*gasping, he whirls round. His nerves are near to cracking*) How the hell did you get back in here?

Darlene (*rising*) I've been here all the time.

Jay (*shocked*) What! I thought you'd climbed out of the window and used the ledge.

Darlene No. I was lying behind the bed—luckily for you. (*Listening*) Is that my phone? (*She hurries to the front door and opens it slightly*)

Jay I don't know. Why don't you go and sit by the ruddy thing?

Darlene (*listening at the door, she shakes her head and closes the door again*) Is that true, what she said?

Jay Please. (*Waving her away*) I want to be alone.

Darlene Alone? What about dog-like devotion in the bathroom?

Jay (*he had forgotten*) Oh God! My mind is going. It's going. You push off while you have the chance.

Jay moves Darlene towards the front door. Before he reaches it, the doorbell rings. Once again he swings Darlene round and heads her back towards the bed. He picks up the control box and closes the curtains

Darlene I'm sick of hiding in here.

54   Do Not Disturb

Jay Then use that window and the ledge. It's quite wide, and it's only a couple of yards to one of your windows.

The doorbell rings again, as Jay approaches the door. He opens the door

Rose stands outside, holding a large pair of scissors. Her hand is raised, in a possibly aggressive gesture

Jay grapples with her, as he did with Sonia

What the hell ...!
Rose Jason!
Jay (*snatching the scissors away from Rose*) What are you doing with these?
Rose I found them on the stairs. I'm sorry if I startled you.
Jay I see. That's all right.
Rose Jason, I must see you.
Jay It's not convenient, Rose.
Rose (*coming in*) Oh, don't say there's someone here?
Jay Um—no but I was running a bath.
Rose Couldn't it wait? Please!
Jay Seems it'll have to. Just a minute. I'll turn it off.

Jay enters the bathroom, squeezing through the door, which he closes behind him

Left alone, Rose looks hungrily at the bottle of gin. She snatches it up, drinks a majestic slug straight from the bottle, then hastily replaces the bottle

Jay comes out of bathroom again a second later

So what can I do for you at this hour?
Rose (*clearly under great stress*) It's—George.
Jay What about him?
Rose When I got home, I found him slumped in a chair, the telephone clutched in his hand ...
Jay (*guiltily*) Telephone!
Rose Rigid, his teeth bared, his eyes staring ... dead.
Jay (*mortified*) Oh, no! God!
Rose I can't describe the—the expression on his face. There was no expression ... It was sort of frozen, and yet there was such hatred, accusation ...
Jay Rose, I don't know what to say. It's the most ghastly thing I ever ...
Rose Then slowly he rose to his feet ...
Jay (*giving a great start*) Wha-at!
Rose And pointed a finger at me.
Jay Just a minute! Stop! What are you trying to say—that he rose from the dead?
Rose I don't understand.
Jay *You* don't understand! Rose, ten seconds ago you said you'd found George dead.
Rose No, I didn't.
Jay You said his teeth were bared, his eyes staring and that he was dead.

Rose Not him. His *eyes*. They looked glassy, dead.

Jay (*vastly relieved and very irritated*) Honestly! I wish you'd choose your words more carefully. I thought I'd ki——I really believed you'd found him dead.

Rose Oh, no. Although I'm surprised he didn't have another stroke. His blood pressure must have been right up. He was in a furious rage.

Jay (*knowing why*) Oh?

Rose He—he found out about my coming here. Don't ask me how.

Jay I won't. But why hadn't you told him, discussed it with him, before you came?

Rose He's a difficult man, Jason. He wouldn't have understood my reasons.

Jay Why not? So you popped in for a totally innocent chat with me. What's so wrong about that?

Rose He always resented you so terribly ...

Jay Why? Because he broke up my marriage?

Rose Because of my guilt feelings which led to—to my problem. (*Indicating the gin bottle*) He went through hell with me until I found salvation. Hardly had we survived that when he had his first stroke. It left him twisted and bitter.

Jay Then isn't it unwise to come straight back here? (*Moving to the window, glancing out*) I know from experience that people hire private detectives.

Rose George won't do anything like that, I promise you.

Jay (*hopefully*) You mean it's forgive and forget, providing we promise never to meet again? (*Sighing suspiciously sincerely*) Well, if that is what he wants ...

Rose (*quietly*) He has thrown me out.

Jay He's what!

Rose He never wants to see me again.

Jay (*with a hint of panic*) You can't be serious.

Rose His sister is coming to look after him. She has never cared for me.

Jay He's out of his mind. What will you do? What's going to happen to you?

Rose You still don't believe in Fate? In a Hand which guides our destiny?

Jay (*carefully*) Guides what, where?

Rose (*suddenly embarrassed*) I ... Jason, I wonder, may I have a drink?

Jay Sure. Coffee or ...?

Rose No—ah—just a wee gin to ...

Jay Rose! (*Registering something*) You've already had one, haven't you? Before you got here?

Rose Yes, I ... it's all been ...

Jay You're a damned fool, Rose. This can kill you and, of course, you're going to blame me because I gave you that wine.

Rose (*shaking her head and slopping some gin into a glass*) No! And don't worry, my dear. Tomorrow I shall be back on the rails; but tonight it's all been a bit too much. (*Gulping neat gin*) I also had to pluck up the courage to come back here. I didn't know what I'd find.

Jay Neither did I.

Rose You're not going back to Sonia, are you?

Jay No, I'm not.

Rose (*squeezing his hand*) Thank goodness! Jason, I would like to stay here tonight.

Jay Would you?

Rose Oh, bless you, my dear!

Jay Hold hard! I didn't say: "Yes", I said: "Would you?" It was a question, not an answer.

Rose May I? Please!

Jay No.

Rose I can't go back to the flat, not tonight.

Jay Then go to a hotel or friends. Nancy Latimer! She'd put you up, and revel in it.

Rose I want to be with you. I need you.

Jay (*controlling himself visibly*) Rose, don't you think it shows an amazing nerve to barge in here, saying you need me, eighteen years after throwing me on the scrap-heap?

Rose I want to make amends, and I think you need me, too.

Jay I don't need anyone.

Rose Let's face it, my dear, now that the physical side is no longer important and we have both reached an age when ...

Jay Stop! Stop right there! I have not "reached" any age, any point of no return. I eagerly anticipate an exciting, invigorating future—and this does not include you and me hunched in front of a fire, sipping Horlicks and discussing your hiatus hernia and my arthritis.

Rose (*eagerly*) You have arthritis?

Jay No! And I'm not catching it to please you.

Rose Dear Jason! (*She slops herself half a tumbler of gin. It may now be possible to detect that alcohol is beginning to affect her. There is care in the pronunciation of words and a slight tendency to tilt*)

Jay (*awed*) Rose, have you seen the size of that gin you just poured?

Rose I can hold my liquor.

Jay But can you hold mine? I don't begrudge the amount, but you're putting away enough to sink a battleship—and I won't have you doing a Mary Rose here.

Rose sinks some more, shakes her head and smiles. She sits in the armchair

Rose You're so plucky.

Jay Plucky?

Rose The brave face you put on things. I know a broken heart does not mend so easily and I understand your scept ... sep ... (*waving her glass*) bitterness. You're probably surprised, shocked that I'm so frank about my feelings, but sometimes, quite clearly, very absolutely clearly, I can see Our Lord's hand at work.

It must be evident to everyone now that Rose is getting very drunk indeed

Jay (*quietly*) He's at it again!

Rose It is written, Jason. All along, all this time. He has meant us to be together.

Jay Earlier on this evening, you extolled the virtues of telling the truth — even if it hurts.

Rose (*waving the glass again, which may slop over*) Absolutely. Oh, absolutely.

Jay now dives in, even though it isn't all that easy. He sits on the end of the sofa, facing Rose

Jay Then, here goes. When you're young everything that happens to you seems utterly irrevocable. Long before George came into your life I was moping around filled with the dread certainty that I shouldn't have married you, that I'd never really been in love with you.

Rose visibly freezes, and puts down the glass with a clatter

Coming as I did from a broken home, I think I'd been looking for a mother figure and the longer we lived together the more like my mother you became. The trouble is, I didn't like my mother very much.

There is a silence. Rose stares at him with big, wide eyes. It is hard to know how she has received this. Jay waits nervously, expecting a violent display of emotion or perhaps collapse

Rose (*at last*) I quite agree. I didn't like her either.

Jay literally falls back into the sofa with his feet momentarily in the air. We hear the distant sound of Darlene's telephone ringing. The curtains round the bed suddenly part. Darlene scampers out and runs to the front door, wrapped in the sheet

Darlene Excuse me. My phone. Could be Sydney.

Darlene exits through the front door

Tilting visibly, Rose watches her go, then turns to look at Jay, who makes an apologetic gesture, but, since there is nothing adequate to say, says nothing

Rose I see. I see. (*Walking with excessive care, she rises and heads inexorably towards the bathroom door*)

Jay (*suddenly realizing he has another crisis (Mary) on his hands*) Rose, where are you going?

Rose To use your bathroom, if I may.

Jay No, you can't.

Rose (*pausing at the door*) Why?

Jay Oh hell. (*Loudly*) Because there's a naked girl in there!

Rose utters a disbelieving laugh, opens the bathroom door and walks straight in, then walks straight out again. As, still walking with care, Rose passes him, Jay makes a helpless gesture as if to say: "Well, I did tell you." Rose now approaches the kitchen door

Now where are you going?

Rose To use your kitchen, if I may.

Jay You can't use the kitchen for . . .

58 (grandly and very distinctly) To make a coff of cuppee, cuff of ... tea.

Rose (*grandly and very distinctly*) To make a coff of cuppee, cuff of ... tea.

Rose enters the kitchen and firmly shuts the door

The phone rings

Mary, wrapped in a towel, emerges from the bathroom during the following conversation. She again collides with the pouffe, but not quite so disastrously

Jay (*answering the phone*) Hullo? ... Yes, it is. Who wants him? ... Hullo? Hullo? Who is this? (*He hangs up*) Odd.

Mary What?

Jay, still nervy, is startled by her and whirls round

Jay Oh, it's you. Some man asked for me then hung up.

Mary Cyril!

Jay You said he didn't know about this place.

Mary I may have made a bit of a boo-boo. He could have found my diary.

Jay (*menacingly*) You kept a diary with this address in it? Well done!

Mary Not the address, only the phone number.

Jay (*slightly relieved*) That's something. They won't give addresses from a phone number, except to the police.

Mary He *is* the police.

Jay What!

Mary I must have told you. I know I have. Special Patrol Group.

Jay That lot? He's probably in that call-box opposite. (*Moving to the window and peeking out*) Checks that I'm in, then comes up with the rubber truncheon which maims without bruising. You're a treasure, Miss Parfitt. (*Approaching Mary; quietly furious*) Still feel sexy? Time for a quickie before the kill?

Mary (*taking him seriously*) You mean that? (*Pointing to the kitchen*) What about ...?

Jay seizes her and pushes her violently into the bathroom

Jay Get dressed!

As Mary disappears into the bathroom there is a crash and an agonized cry

(*Beginning to crack*) For crying out loud!

Mary hops out of the bathroom

Mary Tripped ... I've twisted my ankle.

Jay Well done again!

Mary You did push me ... aah!

Jay We've got to get you out of here.

Jay starts to help her to walk. A crash of breaking crockery from the kitchen causes Jay to start nervously and release Mary who falls prone in front of the sofa

The kitchen door opens and Rose comes out. She still maintains her dignity, but, basically, is very drunk indeed. She holds a saucer in one hand but no cup. She waves this hand, grandly. The saucer flies away as she waves

Rose Please! Don't get up for me.

Jay She can't get up for anyone. She's hurt her ankle.

Rose (*moving forward; assuming the mantle of the nurse*) I'm a nurse. Which ankle?

Mary The right one. Hullo again.

Rose drops rather suddenly to her knees us *of Mary. She professionally puts both hands to Mary's ankle*

Rose This may be painful.

Rose's fingers start to probe the ankle. This causes her to bend further forward. Her torso continues slowly and inexorably to move, until she topples right over, in slow motion. Finally, she collapses across Mary and passes out cold, with her head lying on the ds *side of Mary's body. Mary struggles weakly*

Jay Rose! Rose! What are you doing? (*Kneeling*) Rose! (*Lifting Rose's head and looking at her face*) I don't believe this. (*Unceremoniously letting Rose's head drop back to the floor*) This can't be happening. It can't.

Mary Squashing me. Aah!

Darlene enters through the front door and sees the strange tableau which could be an orgy of some kind. She has changed into a man's shirt

Darlene (*squeaking*) Oooh!

Jay (*to Darlene*) Ah. You. Give me a hand.

Jay starts to lift Rose up. Darlene assists him

Darlene What . . .?

Jay Never mind what. Shove her on the sofa.

Darlene and Jay dump Rose unceremoniously on the sofa, where she lies with her eyes closed

(*Indicating Mary*) Bathroom with this one.

Mary gives Darlene a puzzled look as Darlene assists Jay in helping her to her feet

Mary Hello, I don't think we . . .

Jay Skip the introductions. How does it feel?

Mary Better, I think. It's going sort of numb.

Jay Can you get yourself dressed?

Mary I can try.

Jay Do that. I want you out of here.

They release Mary, who hops into the bathroom

(*To Darlene*) Thanks for the streaking act. It helped tremendously.

Darlene I had to answer my phone, didn't I? It might have been Sydney.

Jay Sydney who? (*He examines the unconscious Rose*)

Darlene Australia. (*Sighing*) But I was too late. If it was him, he'd rung off.

Jay Your own fault. You could have been there if you'd used the window as I told you.

Darlene It was too dark. I could have killed myself.

Jay I thought that was your ambition. I wonder you didn't jump at the chance.

Darlene I was right the first time. You are hard. (*Looking at Rose*) Poor woman.

Jay Pathetic; a hopeless alcoholic.

Darlene (*accusingly*) It's what you made her, did to her.

Jay Why, here comes Mrs Freud!

Darlene You can laugh but your Sonia was right. You think you're treated badly but it's the other way round, always, with everyone.

Jay Naturally!

Darlene It's true. The one who killed herself, her in there with her leg bust and her marriage up the spout.

Jay Oh, go to hell . . .

Mary (*off*) Aah! Could someone help? I can't . . .

Darlene pushes rudely past Jay and enters the bathroom

Jay has been finally stripped of his sang froid and acts rather like a hurt child, sitting glumly on the pouffe

Jay It's bloody marvellous. (*Gesturing to Rose*) Did I walk out on you? Did I drive you to the bottle? Did I give George his clotted arteries? Suddenly Janet is "the one who killed herself". Who says so? Did the coroner? And you in there, with your leg. Did I stuff my card up your bra? Did I turn a casual romp in the office into Romeo and Juliet? I came here in a last, despairing effort to make a new life, to live a quiet, inoffensive existence of my own design. (*To Rose*) Did I ask you to barge in here to save my soul? Did I invite Sonia? Or you in there? No, I just wanted peace and quiet. I still want that. I won't let it be destroyed. I won't.

Darlene comes out of the bathroom

Darlene You mess up everything and everyone. You're bad news. A jinx. It's scary.

Jay Oh f——

A distant phone rings

Darlene rushes out of the front door, leaving it open, and runs into her own flat

Rose makes a moaning noise, stirs, then slowly sits up

Rose, are you all right?

Rose (*rising unsteadily*) All right? Oh, yes! Rose is all right. But you—poor Jason. You're the sad one. What a lonely old man you're going to be. (*She moves a somewhat uneven path towards the front door*)

Jay Rose . . .

Rose (*turning, holding up one hand*) Please! You don't want me. George doesn't want me; but I know *he'll* take me in.

Jay Jesus.

Rose No. Mr Murphy.

Rose weaves her way out of the front door and moves towards the stairs, leaving the door open

Mary appears at the bathroom door, dressed, after a fashion. She has failed to put on her right shoe, which she carries. She manages to hobble along, putting very little weight on the right foot

Mary Sorry. My visit seems to have ...
Jay (*expansively*) Don't apologize, my darling. I'm eternally grateful to you.
Mary (*optimistically*) Really? Why?
Jay You have taught me in half an hour something which millions of men take a lifetime to discover and then don't really like to face.
Mary Oh, what?
Jay That there's no such thing as a simple screw. Bless you for making it clear so early in my new life. (*Putting his arms on her shoulders and kissing her*) Don't come in to the office tomorrow.
Mary Oh, yes, I'll be fine ...
Jay You're fired.
Mary (*flabbergasted*) Fired? Why?
Jay Pick any reason from ten. Come on.

He helps her towards the front door

Mary I can understand things are a bit tricky but we can still meet ...
Jay No.
Mary Why not?
Jay I'm giving up sex and starting to smoke again. It's safer.
Mary I know you don't mean it. You couldn't after what we had today. (*She halts, wincing with pain*) Ouch! I think you'd better drive me to the nearest hospital.
Jay I'm not driving you anywhere. Get a taxi. There's a rank round the corner.
Mary (*shocked*) Oh, I say, but ...
Jay That thug of yours could be lurking outside waiting to smash my skull. I'll take you as far as the hall. After you've gone I intend to lock and bolt the door below.
Mary But how am I going to get to the taxi? I can't walk.
Jay Then hop.

Jay and Mary move through the front door

Mary God. I love it when you're brutal.

Jay and Mary disappear downstairs. The door of Darlene's flat opens and Darlene appears. She runs into Jay's flat looking really happy

Darlene Do you know what? (*She sees the room is empty and moves towards the half-open bathroom door*) I say ... thingy ... Willie ... (*She looks into the bathroom*)

Darlene enters the kitchen

(Off) Are you there?

Jay comes up the stairs and turns towards Darlene's flat. As he speaks, Darlene comes out of the kitchen and listens

Jay Hey! Miss Knickerless Wonder. It's your favourite jinx. Oy! Mrs Freud! Methusalah here. I must be crazy, but I feel like company—even yours.

Darlene sneezes. Jay hears this. He is not a man given to showing emotions but we can see Jay is pleased to see Darlene

Oh. You're there.

Darlene Do you know what? That was him on the phone, and I'm leaving tomorrow for Australia. *(Suddenly, for the first time, she looks positively radiant)*

Jay Good on yer, sport! Let's have a cosy drink to celebrate ...

Clearly Darlene is not meaning to be brusque or hurtful, she is just saying "bye-bye" to a casual aquaintance

Darlene Can't now. *(Going to the door)* Got to go to my mum's to pick up the rest of my gear, so it's goodbye. *(She waves)*

Darlene goes, leaving the door open, and exits to her own flat

Jay Bye. *(He stands for a moment or two. He closes the front door, perhaps locking it. He then carries out a series of manoeuvres, of a man who doesn't know what the hell to do. He switches on the hi-fi, to play a cassette. He kicks the pouffe into a different position. He looks in the mirror, long and hard, at his own reflection—and he doesn't much like what he sees. Finally, he goes to the phone, taps out a number and waits. After a pause, on the phone)* Hullo? Mother? Was it you who liked cold vindaloo?

CURTAIN

FURNITURE AND PROPERTY LIST

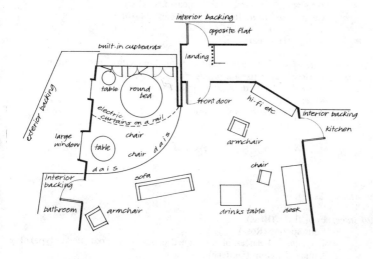

ACT I

On stage: Rolls of wall paper
Pots of paint
Step ladder
Suitcase. *In it:* clothes, men's underpants, one white pair with "Big Willie" in red on the front
Tea chest. *In it:* objects wrapped in newspaper, a whistle
Mirror
Shelves. *On them:* hi-fi, books, ornaments, broken clock
Desk. *On it:* push-button telephone, telephone directories, tumblers, pocket-tape recorder, gin, whisky, pencil, paper
Pouffe
Sofa
Armchair. *On it:* cushions. *Behind it:* pile of plates, one in two pieces
Coffee table. *On it:* ash tray
Round bed. *On it:* pillows, sheet, duvet
Small table. *On it:* lamp
Dining-table. *On it:* remote control instrument for curtains (curtains operated manually by **stage management**)
Four chairs

Off stage: Paper bag. *In it:* loaf of rye bread **(Darlene)**
            Empty box **(Jay)**
            Empty champagne bottle **(Jay)**
            Dishcloth **(Jay)**
            Brown carrier bag. *In it:* chicken and chips in cartons **(Darlene)**
            White carrier bag. *In it:* Chinese food in cartons **(Sonia)**
            Bottle of rice wine **(Sonia)**
            Briefcase. *In it:* Greek food in cartons **(Mary)**
            Carrier bag. *In it:* Indian food in cartons **(Rose)**
            Tray **(Sonia)**
            Trolley **(Darlene)**

Personal: **Jay:** wristwatch, diary, wallet containing credit cards, pound note
            Darlene: paper tissues, pound note, 2 pill bottles
            Sonia: handbag containing cigarettes, lighter
            Rose: handbag
            Mary: thick-lensed spectacles

ACT II

SCENE 1

On stage: As before

Off stage: Four forks **(Rose)**
            Four spoons **(Rose)**
            Tray. *On it:* 4 glasses, plates, large dish, full pepper pot (shaker type) **(Jay)**
            Tomato ketchup **(Darlene)**
            Water jug **(Darlene)**

Personal: **Mary:** thick-lensed spectacles

SCENE 2

On stage: As before

Off stage: Mug **(Jay)**
            Large scissors **(Sonia)**
            Band-Aid **(Jay)**
            Large scissors **(Rose)**
            Shoe **(Mary)**

LIGHTING PLOT

Property fittings required: nil

Interior. A flat. The same scene throughout

ACT I.   Late afternoon

To open: General interior lighting

No cues

ACT II, SCENE 1.   As close of previous Act

Cue 1   **Jay** and **Darlene** stand looking at each other   (Page 46)
            Fade to Black-out

ACT II, SCENE 2

To open: Dim night light from windows, and electric light from kitchen

Cue 2   **Jay** turns on the room lights   (Page 46)
            Snap on sitting-room lighting

EFFECTS PLOT

ACT I

Cue 1	**Jay** presses a button *Alcove curtains start to close with a pleasant hum*	(Page 2)
Cue 2	**Jay** presses another button *Alcove curtains open*	(Page 2)
Cue 3	**Jay** lies down on the bed and starts to close the curtains *Alcove curtains start to close*	(Page 2)
Cue 4	**Jay** stops the curtains *Alcove curtains stop*	(Page 2)
Cue 5	After **Darlene** has entered the kitchen *Crashing noise*	(Page 2)
Cue 6	**Jay:** Axe? Gun? *Doorbell rings*	(Page 4)
Cue 7	**Jay:** "… youthful irresponsibility?" *Phone rings*	(Page 7)
Cue 8	**Jay:** "Never think so, would you?" *Doorbell rings*	(Page 12)
Cue 9	**Jay:** "… in one of the columns." *Doorbell rings*	(Page 13)
Cue 10	**Jay:** "… a dirty old man." *Letter-box flap bangs*	(Page 17)
Cue 11	**Darlene:** "… you're a dirty old man." *Letter-box flap bangs*	(Page 17)
Cue 12	**Jay:** "Too much!" *Doorbell rings*	(Page 17)
Cue 13	**Rose:** "… to the happiness of your soul." *Doorbell rings*	(Page 23)
Cue 14	**Jay:** "Live for now." *Brief, loud explosion*	(Page 26)
Cue 15	**Jay** closes the curtains using the remote control *Alcove curtains close*	(Page 26)
Cue 16	**Jay** opens the curtains again *Alcove curtains open*	(Page 27)
Cue 17	**Jay:** "… lose a friend." *Thumping crash*	(Page 28)
Cue 18	**Jay:** "… a little peace and quiet?" *Doorbell rings*	(Page 29)